00-00000-0 [to be assigned]

his book contains general guidance only and does
legal, financial, or specialist professional advice.
ld obtain independent professional advice for their
mstances. Laws, regulations, and tariff rates
s verify current requirements before committing to
saction.

by the author

INTERNATIONAL T

IN

The Ins

Internat

Published by Johr

Part of the Interna

First published Ju

Second Edition p

ISBN 978-0-

Disclaimer: T
not constitute
Readers sho
specific circ
change; alwa
any trade tra

Cover design

About the International Trade and Transport Law Library

This book is the first volume in the International Trade and Transport Law Library, published under the John Gates Books imprint. The series provides practitioners, entrepreneurs, and students with authoritative, experience-based guidance on the legal, commercial, and practical dimensions of moving goods across international borders.

Each volume stands independently, but the series rewards readers who move through it in sequence. This first volume maps the territory. Later books address specialist topics in greater technical depth.

Books in the Series

Book One: International Trade — The Ins and Outs of Import and Export (this volume)

Book Two: Bills of Lading in Shipping Law: An Australian Perspective

Book Three: Marine Insurance – An Australian Perspective

Further volumes in preparation.

Readers who need detailed legal analysis of bills of lading, carrier liability under the Hague-Visby Rules, or the Carriage of

Goods by Sea Act 1991 (Cth) are referred to Book Two in this series.

Foreword

People have been trading across borders for as long as there have been borders. Before there was money, there was barter. Before there were ships, there were rivers. The principles underlying international trade have not changed much since those early days: you have something someone else wants; they have something you need — usually money. The challenge is getting the goods from one place to another safely, legally, at a profit, and without either party being cheated.

Simple in theory.

In practice, it is one of the most complex commercial undertakings a person can attempt.

I spent a significant part of my career as a cargo lawyer, and later with one of the world's largest inspection agencies. In that time I watched extraordinary transactions succeed brilliantly, and I watched brave, intelligent, hard-working people lose everything — not because they lacked drive, but because they encountered risks they simply did not know existed.

That observation became the theme of this book, and the mantra that runs through it from first page to last:

"You don't know what you don't know."

The risks you know about are manageable. You can insure against them, plan for them, price them in, or walk away. It is the risks you do not know about — the unknown unknowns — that can destroy a deal, a business, or in the most serious cases, cause real personal harm to the people involved.

International trade is also, I should say clearly, one of the most rewarding and exciting things you can do in business. Every deal is different. Every country is different. Every cargo tells a story. The opportunity to build genuine commercial relationships across cultures and continents is one that previous generations of traders did not have in anything like the same measure.

This book is for the entrepreneur who is ready to have a go. Read it as a map, not a manual. Use it to know what questions to ask, where the deep water is, and when you need a skilled guide beside you. Then get out there.

The world is waiting for what you have to offer.

John Gates
Brisbane, Queensland, Australia, 2025

A Note on This Book

This is a book of general guidance, not legal or financial advice. Although I practised for many years as an International Trade and Transport Lawyer, nothing in this book should be taken as legal advice for your specific circumstances. Laws, regulations, tariff rates, trade agreements, and customs requirements change constantly, and vary enormously between jurisdictions.

Before making any significant trade transaction — signing a contract, shipping a cargo, opening a letter of credit, or entering a new market — please obtain specific professional advice. A good lawyer at the exporting end, and a good lawyer at the importing end, will pay for themselves many times over.

The anecdotes in this book are drawn from real experience. They are included not as warnings but as illustrations of how the principles work in practice — and occasionally how they fail when ignored.

"You don't know what you don't know."

Contents

PART ONE

The World Out There

Understanding the territory before you start

CHAPTER 1

The Nature of Doing Business Across Borders

Let me begin with the most important thing I learned as a cargo lawyer, and the thing I saw violated — catastrophically — more times than I can count.

"You don't know what you don't know."

Australia is, in many respects, a wonderful place from which to do business. We operate under a coherent legal system, a trustworthy banking framework, reliable government agencies, and a culture of commercial honesty we tend to take entirely for granted. We assume, unconsciously, that these conditions are universal. They are not.

Step off a plane in certain parts of the world, and the rules change immediately. Not subtly. Completely. The moment you set foot on foreign soil you become subject to the laws of that country — fiscal law, customs law, import and export regulations, currency controls, business registration requirements, and rules about what you can say, promise, advertise, and claim about your goods. None of that is automatically consistent with what you know at home.

What Makes International Trade Different

Most domestic businesses manage risk quite well, because the risk environment is familiar. Your bank knows you. Your lawyer knows the local courts. Your accountant understands the tax system. The culture of business is the one you grew up in.

International trade strips all of that away. Suddenly you are doing business with people you have never met, in a legal system you have not studied, often in a language you do not speak, across a physical distance that makes oversight difficult and swift intervention nearly impossible. The transaction involves more participants than a domestic sale — freight forwarders, customs brokers, inspection agencies, overseas banks, carriers, and agents — each of whom introduces their own potential for error, delay, or misconduct. Every link in that chain is a potential point of failure.

The Perception of Risk

If you are completely risk-averse, international trade may not be for you. That is not an invitation to recklessness. It is a recognition that every international transaction contains risk that cannot be entirely eliminated — only understood, managed, and priced. The successful international trader does not refuse risk. They catalogue it, analyse it, mitigate what can be mitigated, insure against what can be insured, and build a price structure that reflects what remains.

They also develop, over time, an instinct for when a deal smells wrong. I once watched a very experienced colleague kill a deal that looked excellent on paper, because something about the counterpart's response to a request for bank references made him uneasy. He could not articulate exactly what bothered him. He just shut it down. Two years later, the counterpart was the subject of an international fraud investigation. That kind of judgment takes time to develop. Until it does, you need knowledge.

Political and Regulatory Risk

The most dramatic risk in international trade is also the most underestimated: the risk that the political or regulatory environment of the target country changes in ways that affect your deal. Wars and coups are obvious, but they are actually among the more manageable risks because they are newsworthy. The subtler political risks are more insidious: a change of government that ushers in new import restrictions; a sudden imposition of currency controls that prevents your buyer from remitting funds; a nationalisation of the industry you were supplying. I have seen each of these happen.

There are also quieter regulatory risks: customs authorities that interpret classification rules in unexpected ways; quarantine requirements that appear at the border without warning; anti-dumping duties applied retrospectively to a product you have been shipping profitably for years. None of these should stop you trading. But they should be on your risk register, and they should influence how you structure every deal.

Legal Risk

The most dangerous assumption in international contracting is that a clause enforceable at home will be enforceable abroad. It will not always be. A jurisdiction clause that sends disputes to Australian courts may be ignored by a court in another country that has never acknowledged foreign judgments. An arbitration clause specifying ICC rules may be of limited practical use if your counterpart's assets are in a country that is not a signatory to the New York Convention on the Recognition and Enforcement of Foreign Arbitral Awards.

Get legal advice from lawyers who know the target jurisdiction, not just lawyers who know your home jurisdiction. Both are necessary. Neither alone is sufficient.

A Framework for Managing Risk

You will never eliminate risk in international trade. You can, however, manage it systematically. My framework has five elements.

Know your trading partner.

Before signing anything, verify who you are dealing with. Obtain credit references. Research the company. If possible, visit the premises. The international trading community is smaller than it appears, and reputations travel.

Use the right professionals.

A good freight forwarder, a good customs broker, and a good trade lawyer at each end of the transaction are not luxuries. Their fees are a fraction of what you stand to lose if something goes wrong without them.

Document everything.

Every agreement, every instruction, every variation should be in writing. A handshake in a hotel lobby is not a contract.

Insure appropriately.

Marine cargo insurance is one of the oldest and most sophisticated branches of the insurance industry. Use it correctly — make sure your broker has the full picture of your cargo, your route, and your risk profile. Discover any policy exclusions before you need to make a claim.

Know when to walk away.

Not every deal is worth doing. Some markets are too politically unstable. Some counterparts are too opaque. Some prices are too good to be true. If it looks like a rat and smells like a rat, do not load it into a container.

CHAPTER 2

The Unknown Unknowns: Why Brave People Fail

International trade has a particular way of humbling the overconfident. I have watched it happen to very smart people — people who were extremely capable in every other commercial context. The common factor was not lack of intelligence or courage. It was lack of specific knowledge in a specific area, and — crucially — lack of awareness that the gap existed.

This chapter is about those gaps. Not the obvious ones. The less obvious ones — the ones that do not appear in the brochures but appear with alarming regularity in the cargo insurance claims files and the admiralty law reports.

The Entrepreneur's Blind Spot

Entrepreneurs are, by definition, people who back themselves. That confidence — the willingness to act on incomplete information, to take calculated risks, to persist when things are difficult — is what makes entrepreneurship possible. But the same confidence that drives an entrepreneur forward can, in an unfamiliar environment, become a liability. The very fact that they have succeeded in their domestic market can create a false sense that the skills and instincts that worked at home will work abroad.

The unknown unknowns are not the things you are wrong about. They are the things you have not thought to ask about.

Stories from the Cargo Hold

The Container That Wasn't Right

The shipping container is the fundamental unit of modern international trade. There are approximately forty million containers in circulation globally. Most are in excellent condition. Some are not. The ones in the worst condition tend to end up on the longest routes, because container owners — many of whom are based in Europe and North America — rotate their best stock through high-frequency short-haul routes and send older equipment on the long hauls.

A voyage from an Australian port to a European destination takes a container through the Southern Ocean, around the Cape of Good Hope or through the Suez Canal, across changes in temperature, barometric pressure, humidity, and sea state that would challenge even a sound container. A small defect — a corroded corner casting, a compromised door seal, a hairline crack in the roof panel — may hold together in calm conditions and fail in heavy weather.

The prudent exporter inspects the container before loading.

Not a casual glance — a proper inspection, by a qualified surveyor, with a written report. It costs a few hundred dollars. The cost of a damaged cargo, a disputed insurance claim, and an unrecoverable receiver's lien is orders of magnitude higher. Most of my clients did not know this until after the event.

The Prawn Story

A client of mine — a sharp, experienced businessman who had been trading domestically for fifteen years — decided to export frozen seafood to the US West Coast. Good product, reliable supply, strong demand. He identified a San Francisco buyer, negotiated a price, arranged the insurance, and booked the freight. What he had not arranged, because he did not know it was necessary, was a pre-shipment inspection of the containers.

The containers were supplied by the carrier and appeared adequate. What a proper inspection would have revealed was minor corrosion around a seam seal in one container — invisible without specialist inspection, but sufficient, over a long Pacific voyage, to admit enough moisture to compromise the reefer unit.

The cargo arrived in San Francisco partially spoiled. US Customs would not allow it to land. The buyer refused it. The insurer disputed the claim on a technical reading of the exclusion clauses. The result was spoiled prawns sitting in a container off the California coast, with demurrage accumulating by the day, no buyer willing to take them, and my client facing the cost of towing the cargo out to sea and disposing of it in accordance with international pollution regulations.

He had done nothing wrong exactly. He had been brave, organised, and commercially astute. He just did not know what he did not know. A single inspection certificate, costing a few hundred dollars, would have identified the container defect before the cargo was ever loaded.

The Interpreter Problem

I once went on a delegation from Canberra to Beijing to negotiate a commercial agreement of some significance. We had prepared carefully: briefing documents, proposed contract framework, the whole package translated into Mandarin. We had engaged what we believed to be an independent interpreter.

Partway through the negotiations, our Chinese counterpart dismissed our interpreter and proposed that a member of their own team serve as translator for both sides. Short questions from us produced long translations. Long questions from our counterpart produced short ones. We could not know what was being communicated, what was being added, and what was being omitted. The deal did not proceed.

The lesson is not that Chinese counterparts are untrustworthy. The lesson is that interpreters in commercial negotiations must be independently engaged, independently verified, and not shared with the other side. This is something that many inexperienced international traders, accustomed to domestic negotiations where everybody speaks the same language, simply do not think about.

The Beautiful Contract That Could Not Be Enforced

A client came to me with a thirty-page commercial agreement he had negotiated with a manufacturer in a provincial Chinese city. It was an excellent contract — beautifully drafted, comprehensive, governing law properly specified, dispute resolution clearly set out. His Sydney lawyer had done superb work.

The problem was the dispute resolution clause. It specified ICC arbitration, seated in Sydney. The Chinese manufacturer had signed it — which, in retrospect, should have been the first warning sign, because an experienced Chinese counterpart would have known that it was effectively worthless.

When the dispute arose — goods bearing no resemblance to the approved samples — my client had a beautifully drafted unenforceable document. Chinese courts do not automatically enforce foreign arbitration awards. A clause specifying Australian jurisdiction was, from the perspective of a court in that provincial city, simply irrelevant. The contract must be enforceable where your counterpart's assets are. I address this in detail in Appendix 3.

The Seller or Investor Problem

There is a trap that catches first-time international traders with a frequency I found remarkable, and it deserves direct treatment.

When you enter a foreign market as a seller — exporting your goods, receiving payment through secure banking channels, and returning home — your exposure is largely manageable. When you enter a foreign market as an investor — putting money into a venture, a manufacturing facility, or a joint venture — your exposure changes entirely. You are now subject to local laws governing foreign investment, property rights, and what happens when a venture fails. In many parts of the world, those laws are not kind to foreign investors.

I visited Myanmar in the early 1990s, when the country was just beginning to open to foreign commerce. Every evening, the bar of the hotel was full of adventurers from a dozen countries, each convinced they had found the deal of the century. Some had been there for months. The deal that had looked imminent when they arrived was still not signed. Their capital was dwindling. The government officials who had seemed so welcoming were now elusive.

My partner and I were in and out in a few days at a time, selling goods, getting paid, leaving. We never sank capital into the market. Others did, and many of them never got it back.

The principle is simple: sell into foreign markets by all means. Use the established mechanisms of international trade — letters of credit, confirmed by reputable banks, in your favour — to ensure you are paid before you lose control of your goods. Do not become a creditor of a foreign jurisdiction when you do not understand it. Do not let enthusiasm substitute for homework.

The Risk of Moving Too Fast

The final unknown unknown is the most common of all: the risk of moving too fast. International trade takes time. Relationships take time. Understanding a market takes time. In some parts of the world, a negotiation that appears to have stalled is, from your counterpart's perspective, proceeding exactly as expected. They are learning about you — assessing your reliability, your patience, your seriousness of purpose. A rushed proposal is an alarm signal.

You will not always know which environment you are in until you have spent time in it with the right guides. This is another reason why experienced local representatives are not an optional extra — they are a fundamental requirement of doing business responsibly in an unfamiliar environment.

CHAPTER 3

Your First Decision: Go It Alone or Use a Trading House?

Before you negotiate with overseas suppliers or buyers, before you select a freight forwarder or approach your bank, there is one strategic decision that will shape everything else: are you going to manage the international side of your business yourself, or are you going to engage a Trading House to do it for you?

What is a Trading House?

A Trading House is a company whose business is facilitating international trade on behalf of other businesses. It does not manufacture, and in most cases, it does not import or export on its own account. Its role is to stand between you and the extraordinary complexity of the international supply chain and manage that complexity on your behalf.

A good Trading House has networks in the markets you want to enter, relationships with reliable freight forwarders, customs brokers, inspection agencies, and banks, knowledge of regulatory requirements in dozens of jurisdictions, experience with the documentation required for international transactions, and the commercial intelligence to identify risks that you would not see yourself.

When you engage a Trading House, your responsibility as a supplier reduces to four things: supply the goods at the agreed quality, in the agreed quantity, at the agreed price, and on the agreed timetable. Everything else — the logistics chain, the banking arrangements, the insurance, the customs clearance, the inspection certificates, the relationship with the overseas counterpart — is the Trading House's problem.

That simplicity has a cost. Trading Houses charge for their services, and the margin you give up by going through an intermediary is real. But so is the alternative cost — the time, the mistakes, the legal exposure, and the sheer cognitive load of managing an international supply chain yourself when you do not yet know what you are doing.

The Case for Using a Trading House

To establish a genuine presence in an overseas market requires a sustained effort of at least two to three years. A dedicated export department will succeed only if management gives it status equal to the domestic sales department and allocates the budgets necessary for long-term development. Most small and medium businesses are not in a position to make that commitment.

In that context, the Trading House offers something valuable: it lets you access international markets without diverting the resources that your core business needs. Your job is to make excellent products. The Trading House's job is to get them to the right buyers, in the right markets, at the right price, with all the paperwork in order. A good Trading House will also be proactive — alerting you to opportunities in markets you had not considered, advising on product adaptation, managing currency risk, and maintaining the long-term relationships with buyers and agents that take years to develop from scratch.

The Case for Going It Yourself

Not everyone should use a Trading House. If your volumes are small, the Trading House margin may make the deal uneconomic. If you have industry-specific knowledge that is genuinely rare, a Trading House may not add the value that a specialist would. If the relationship with the overseas counterpart is central to your business model, delegating it to an intermediary may not be appropriate.

There are also businesses for which the international experience is itself the objective — companies that want to build genuine international capability and are prepared to accept that the early years will be expensive and imperfect in order to build something proprietary.

A Middle Path

In practice, many businesses end up on a middle path: they engage a Trading House for their first few transactions, use that experience to learn the landscape, and then gradually bring more of the function in-house as their knowledge and confidence grow. The Trading House becomes, in effect, an expensive but practical education.

At some point, you will be able to replicate most of what the Trading House does. But you will probably still use specialist intermediaries for specific tasks — customs classification questions, unusual cargo requirements, complex letter of credit negotiations — because the expertise remains valuable even when you are no longer dependent on it.

Choosing a Trading House

If you decide to use a Trading House, choose one with genuine expertise in your product sector and your target market. A Trading House that is excellent in the Asia-Pacific agricultural commodities space may be of limited use if you are exporting manufactured goods to the Middle East. Check their references carefully. Talk to other exporters they have represented. Understand exactly what services they will provide and what they will not, and make sure the commercial terms — their fees, their margin structure, their liability position — are clearly documented.

The Australian Government's Austrade network, your bank's international trade desk, and industry associations in your sector are all useful starting points for identifying appropriate intermediaries. Do not select a Trading House on price alone. In international trade, as in most things, you get what you pay for.

PART TWO

Before You Begin

Research, planning, and product readiness

CHAPTER 4

Market Research: Finding Where You Fit

Most traders who walked into trouble had one thing in common: they had spent their time and energy on the deal itself — the product, the price, the negotiation — and not enough time on understanding the environment in which the deal would have to work. Market research is the single most important thing you can do before committing any resources to an international venture.

Start with the Market, Not the Product

The discipline of market research asks you to look at your product through the market's eyes, not your own. The question is not "what do I have?" but "what does this market need, and does my product meet that need in a way that is commercially viable?" A product that sells beautifully in the Australian market may need modification, rebranding, repackaging, or repositioning to be competitive elsewhere. In some markets it may have no viable place at all.

Identifying a Viable Market

When assessing a potential market, three conditions must be met. The market must be large enough, and growing enough, to sustain your commercial objectives. The market must be open and competitive enough to allow a new entrant to establish a position. And the country must be financially solvent enough that your buyer can actually pay.

Beyond these fundamentals, assess the practical accessibility of the market: the quality of the banking system, the reliability of the legal system as it applies to foreign commercial parties, the infrastructure for freight and logistics, and the availability of trustworthy local agents.

The Market Study in Practice

A proper market study has two stages. The first is desk research — everything you can find out without leaving home. The second is field research — what you learn by actually being in the market.

Desk research begins with the country briefs available from Austrade, supplemented by the World Bank's Doing Business reports, industry association publications, and the publicly available trade statistics that most governments publish. You are looking for: the size and growth trajectory of the market for your product type; the competitive landscape, including the countries that are the principal current suppliers; the tariff and regulatory environment; and the credit and political risk profile of the country.

Field research means going to the market. No amount of desk research substitutes for physical presence. The meetings, the visits to trade shows, the conversations with local agents and importers, the walk through a retail district to see how products like yours are displayed and priced — these things reveal what databases cannot. I was in New Delhi in 1996 with a colleague assessing a senior marketing role with an international pharmaceutical company. What our desk research had not prepared us for was the distribution system. There were no supermarkets or warehouse chains as we understood them. The market was real. The opportunity was real. But the operational model required to address it was entirely different from what worked in Australia. He passed on the opportunity. He was right to do so.

Adapting Your Product

Success in one market does not guarantee success in another. Adaptation may be as simple as a change of labelling, or it may require substantive changes to the product itself to meet local regulatory requirements, cultural preferences, or distribution norms.

In the North American market, the demands are particularly exacting. The US consumer market is the largest and most sophisticated in the world, and the expectations around product quality, liability, and supply chain consistency are correspondingly high. If you miss a supply commitment or fall below quality standards, you may not get a second chance. Many exporters find that the US market requires a level of operational scale and reliability that they cannot achieve from a small manufacturing base. Licensing the product to a local manufacturer may be a more realistic path.

Make these assessments before you commit to the market, not after. Adaptation costs money and time. If the adaptation required to make your product competitive in a target market makes the deal uneconomic, it is better to know that upfront and look elsewhere.

Know Your Product — Really

Before you take your product to a foreign market, you need to understand it in ways that go well beyond its performance characteristics. You need to know: whether it requires regulatory approval, safety certification, health registration, environmental compliance, or import permits in the target market; whether it is subject to quarantine requirements; its correct Harmonised System classification, because that determines the tariff rate it attracts; and whether any of its components are subject to trade controls or sanctions restrictions.

You also need to be honest about whether you can supply the market consistently. A large market may want quantities you cannot reliably produce. A demanding market may want quality standards your current production process does not meet. Identify these constraints before you have made commitments.

The Pre-Launch Checklist

Before progressing to the operational stage, you should be able to answer yes to each of the following:

- I have identified a specific target market and verified there is genuine demand for my product.
- I have assessed the competitive landscape and believe I have a viable commercial advantage.
- I have verified the HS classification of my product and the duty rates that apply in the target market.
- I have checked for import permits, quarantine requirements, and regulatory approvals my product requires.

- I have assessed the political and financial risk of the target country.
- I have identified trustworthy local representatives or agents in the market.
- I have done my numbers — including all logistics, insurance, tariff, and adaptation costs — and the deal is commercially viable at a realistic sale price.
- I have planned my first visit to the market.

If you cannot yet answer yes to all of these, more homework is required. The time it takes to do this properly is not lost time — it is the time that separates traders who succeed from those who learn these lessons the expensive way.

CHAPTER 5

Protecting Your Intellectual Property

If your product has something unique about it — a formula, a design, a brand, a manufacturing process — you need to decide, early in your export planning, how much you are prepared to spend protecting it, and how realistic that protection is in the markets you intend to enter.

I say "how realistic" deliberately, because one of the most painful unknown unknowns I observed in my career was the trader who spent years and significant capital securing patent and trademark protection, only to discover that in the markets that mattered most to them, that protection was either unenforceable or irrelevant.

The Window of Opportunity

In technology-driven and fashion-driven markets, the appropriate question about IP protection is not "how do I protect this forever?" but "how long do I have before this is copied, and how do I maximise my returns in that window?"

If your product is going to be a market-changer, the speed with which you get it to market and establish distribution is often worth more than the time you spend perfecting your legal defences. Consider the toy market — the Rubik's Cube, the fidget spinner, the yo-yo in its many reinventions. People made fortunes from these products for limited periods. The ones who won were the ones who moved fast, got distribution, and had already moved to the next product by the time the copies arrived.

If your product is a long-term play — a pharmaceutical, a proprietary manufacturing process, a genuinely unique technology — then the investment in comprehensive IP protection is justified. The answer depends on the product.

Patents and Trademarks

Patent and trademark protection is the traditional approach, and it remains the best tool available for products that warrant it. In Australia, the starting point is IP Australia (ipaustralia.gov.au), which administers patents, trademarks, and designs. For international protection, the Patent Cooperation Treaty (PCT) provides a streamlined mechanism for filing patent applications across multiple jurisdictions simultaneously.

Be realistic about the lead times involved. A patent application from filing to grant can take several years. The IP landscape in your target market needs to be researched early — ideally before you finalise your product design — because the discovery that someone has already registered your proposed trademark in the target market, or that a similar patent has been granted, is a very painful one to make after you have invested in production and marketing.

Reverse Engineering

Reverse engineering will happen.

In many parts of the world, it is not even regarded as ethically problematic. Somebody will analyse your formula, or your design, and make it look like theirs. They will be well funded, because you paid for the R&D. All they have to do is pay a few chemists or engineers to re-create what you have made, and then market it — often in your target market, where they have production cost advantages and established distribution that you are still trying to build.

A troll around Alibaba or AliExpress at any given moment will reveal hundreds of examples of products that bear a suspicious resemblance to innovations that originated elsewhere. In many jurisdictions, this is simply accepted practice.

Your response must be agility. Stay ahead of the copies by continuing to innovate. Build your brand loyalty before the copies arrive. Secure distribution arrangements that give you shelf presence and customer relationships that the copyists cannot easily replicate. And, where you can enforce your rights, do so

— but be realistic about the cost and likelihood of success in any given jurisdiction.

Confidentiality and Trade Secrets

For certain types of competitive advantage — a unique manufacturing process, a proprietary formula, a customer list, a negotiating strategy — the best protection is simply not to disclose. Tight confidentiality agreements with employees, agents, and joint venture partners, combined with a culture of operational security, can be more effective than legal protection in jurisdictions where legal protection is weak.

If you are sharing technical information with a foreign manufacturer or joint venture partner — which you may have to do in order to produce locally — get comprehensive confidentiality and non-compete obligations in writing, and get local legal advice on whether they are enforceable in the jurisdiction where your partner operates. An NDA governed by Australian law may be of limited comfort when the breach occurs in a country whose courts have no obligation to give it effect.

CHAPTER 6

Finding Your Supplier or Buyer

Whether you are an importer looking for a supplier or an exporter looking for a buyer, the quality of the counterpart you choose will determine, more than almost anything else, whether the transaction succeeds. A good counterpart can compensate for many other weaknesses in a deal. A bad counterpart will make a good deal go wrong.

For Importers: Finding the Right Supplier

If you are importing, you probably know the niche and the type of product you want to bring in. The challenge is identifying the right supplier within that niche — one who is a genuine manufacturer rather than a middleman, who can supply the quality and quantity you need consistently, who has the production capacity to scale with your business, and who is financially stable enough to be a reliable long-term partner.

Online directories have made supplier discovery much easier than it was a generation ago. The major Chinese platforms — Alibaba, AliExpress, and Made-in-China.com — list thousands of suppliers across virtually every product category. They are a useful starting point, but they require critical evaluation. The glossy product photos on a supplier's profile page may not be their own. The ratings and reviews may not tell the full story. The distinction between a genuine manufacturer and a trading company acting as a middleman is not always obvious.

For non-Chinese suppliers, the global directories Salehoo and Worldwide Brands provide curated lists of verified manufacturers, wholesalers, and distributors, with ratings and contact details. These are particularly useful for finding reputable suppliers in markets where the Chinese platforms have limited coverage. There are others, and we recommend that you do the research.

Trade fairs are among the most efficient ways to meet suppliers face to face. The major trade exhibitions in Guangzhou, Shenzhen, and Hong Kong attract manufacturers from across Asia.

Regional shows in your own city regularly attract overseas suppliers who are looking for Australian distributors. A few days at the right trade fair can accomplish more than months of email correspondence.

Inspection and Quality Assurance

Once you have identified a supplier and negotiated terms, do not assume that the goods you receive will match the samples you approved. This is one of the most predictable and consistently underestimated risks in international trade, particularly when sourcing from markets where quality standards are variable.

The solution is a pre-shipment inspection. Companies such as SGS, Bureau Veritas, and Intertek have offices in virtually every major port city in the world and can inspect your goods at the supplier's premises before they are loaded. They will compare the goods against the approved specification, check quantities, verify labelling compliance, and issue a written report. If the goods do not meet the specification, you find out before they are on a ship — not when they arrive at your warehouse six weeks later, too late to do anything practical about it.

I spent time working with SGS, and the anecdotes from that period are instructive. The furniture trader who approved a sample at a trade fair and received a container load of goods assembled with substandard adhesives.

The apparel importer who discovered that the garments in the container bore no resemblance to the samples in terms of fabric weight and construction.

The electronics importer whose goods arrived with the wrong power specifications for the Australian market.

All of these outcomes were preventable with a pre-shipment inspection. None of them occurred in the presence of one.

The cost of a pre-shipment inspection is a few hundred to a few thousand dollars, depending on the size and complexity of the consignment. The cost of receiving a container of non-conforming goods is the cost of the goods, the freight, the duty, the storage, and the disposal — plus the lost sales, the unhappy customers, and the damage to your reputation. The arithmetic is straightforward.

For Exporters: Finding the Right Buyer

If you are exporting, the challenge is identifying buyers in the target market who have genuine demand for your product, the financial capacity to pay for it, and the commercial reliability to honour their obligations.

The Austrade network is an underutilised resource. Austrade trade commissioners are based in markets around the world and have direct knowledge of local industry, local buyers, and local regulatory requirements. They can make introductions, validate potential buyers, and provide market intelligence that would take you months to develop independently. Use them.

Trade missions — organised by governments, industry associations, or chambers of commerce — provide a structured and cost-effective way to enter a new market. You travel as part of a group, which provides credibility and logistical support; you are introduced to pre-vetted potential buyers and government officials; and you leave with a set of contacts and a level of market knowledge that would be much harder to acquire independently.

However you identify potential buyers, verify them before you commit to a transaction. Obtain trade references. Run a credit check through an international credit agency. Ask your bank's international trade desk to verify the buyer's bank standing. In markets where personal relationships are the foundation of commercial trust, invest the time to build those relationships before you ship goods on open account terms.

The letter of credit — which I describe in Part Three — exists precisely because not every buyer can be trusted, and sometimes even trustworthy buyers face circumstances beyond their control.

PART THREE

The Commercial Framework

Contracts, payment, and protecting what you are owed

CHAPTER 7

The International Contract

Everything in international trade flows from the contract. It defines what you have agreed to supply or purchase, on what terms, at what price, with what documentation, and what happens when something goes wrong. A well-drafted international contract will not prevent every problem, but it will give you a framework for resolving them. A poorly drafted one will make every problem worse.

The Basics of a Good International Contract

The fundamental requirements of any commercial contract apply in international trade as they do domestically: you need the parties clearly identified, a clear description of what is being bought and sold, a price and payment mechanism, delivery terms, and the consequences of non-performance. In international trade, several additional elements become critical.

The governing law clause specifies which country's law applies to the interpretation and enforcement of the contract. This matters because commercial law differs significantly between jurisdictions, and the same contractual language can be interpreted very differently by courts in different countries.

The jurisdiction or dispute resolution clause specifies where disputes will be resolved. The choice is typically between litigation in the courts of a specified country, or arbitration under a specified set of rules (such as the ICC Rules or the Singapore International Arbitration Centre rules). Arbitration is generally preferred in international transactions because arbitral awards are more readily enforceable across borders than court judgments, under the New York Convention.

The force majeure clause addresses what happens when a party is prevented from performing by events beyond their control — natural disasters, government actions, pandemics. The scope of this clause became the subject of enormous commercial dispute during the COVID-19 pandemic, and it deserves careful drafting.

The language clause specifies the governing language of the contract. If the contract will need to be enforced in a jurisdiction where a different language is spoken, the contract should ideally be prepared in both languages, with the governing language clearly specified.

Plain English Drafting

There is a movement, which I broadly endorse, towards plain English drafting of commercial contracts. Contracts written in accessible, unambiguous language are less likely to be misunderstood by the parties, less likely to give rise to interpretation disputes, and more likely to reflect the genuine commercial intention of both sides.

However, plain English is not the same as simple.

International commercial contracts address genuinely complex situations, and the language that describes them must be precise. The goal is to be clear without sacrificing accuracy — not to dumb down the document to the point where important nuances are lost.

My advice: start with a template from a reputable source — the International Trade Centre model contracts described in Appendix 4 are an excellent starting point — and then have it reviewed by lawyers who know both your home jurisdiction and the target jurisdiction. Use the template to understand the structure and the scope of the issues to be addressed. Do not use it as a finished product without expert review.

Incoterms: The Language of Delivery

Incoterms are not the contract. They are a standardised vocabulary for one element of the contract: the delivery terms — specifically, where risk and cost pass from seller to buyer in the physical supply chain.

Published by the International Chamber of Commerce and currently in their 2020 edition, Incoterms provide eleven defined terms, each represented by a three-letter acronym.

The most commonly used in Australian international trade are EXW (Ex Works), FOB (Free on Board), CIF (Cost Insurance Freight), and DAP (Delivered at Place). Each has a precise meaning regarding which party bears the cost and risk of transport at each stage of the supply chain.

EXW is the simplest from the seller's perspective — the seller makes the goods available at their own premises, and the buyer arranges everything from there. It places the maximum burden on the buyer, which means it is often inappropriate when the buyer is in a foreign country and unfamiliar with the export requirements of the seller's market.

FOB is the traditional maritime term. Risk and cost pass from seller to buyer when the goods are loaded on board the vessel at the named port of shipment. It is appropriate for full container loads but not for LCL (less than container load) shipments or air freight, where a different point of handover is more appropriate.

CIF means the seller covers the cost of the goods, the insurance, and the freight to the named destination port. Risk still passes to the buyer when the goods are loaded on board the vessel at the port of origin. CIF gives the seller more control over the freight and insurance arrangements, but means the seller is organising logistics in the import country, where they may have less knowledge and leverage than the buyer.

DAP (Delivered at Place) means the seller delivers the goods to a named destination, ready for unloading, and bears all costs and risks up to that point except import duties. It is broadly the opposite of EXW in terms of obligation allocation, and places the maximum burden on the seller.

Choosing the right Incoterm is a commercial decision that requires understanding your product, your logistics chain, your relationship with the buyer, and the banking arrangements being used. The full Incoterms 2020 framework, with detailed guidance on each term, is available from the ICC at iccwbo.org. The detailed treatment of each term from the first edition of this book is reproduced in Appendix 5 for reference.

Negotiation

The negotiation of an international commercial contract is itself a skill that takes years to develop. A few principles are worth stating clearly here.

Know what you need, not just what you want. There will be elements of the contract that are genuinely non-negotiable for commercial or legal reasons — the payment terms, the product specification, the governing law. Distinguish these from the elements that are genuinely negotiable, and be prepared to show flexibility on the latter in exchange for firmness on the former.

Do not rush. The pressure to close — from your own impatience, from the counterpart's apparent eagerness, from a deadline that may or may not be real — is one of the most common causes of poorly considered contracts. Take the time you need to review every clause with your lawyer, particularly the dispute resolution and governing law provisions.

Understand the cultural context. Negotiating styles vary enormously across cultures. In some contexts, a rapid and decisive negotiation is a sign of mutual trust and commercial seriousness. In others, a long and careful process of building relationship and consensus is expected, and a rushed approach is a sign of bad faith. Your local representative or Austrade contact can advise on what to expect in a specific market.

CHAPTER 8

Getting Paid: Trade Finance and Payment Mechanisms

The greatest risk in any international transaction is not being paid. Everything else — the logistics, the quality assurance, the insurance — is ultimately in service of one objective: receiving your money, in full, on time, in a currency you can use. This chapter explains the main mechanisms by which that objective is pursued, and the risks associated with each.

The Letter of Credit

The irrevocable, confirmed Letter of Credit (L/C) is the gold standard of international trade payment mechanisms, and has been for more than a century. If you are selling to a new buyer, in a market you do not know well, under a governing law that provides limited protection to foreign creditors, the letter of credit is your best friend.

The mechanism works as follows. The buyer instructs their bank (the issuing bank) to issue a letter of credit in the seller's favour, specifying the conditions under which payment will be made — typically, the presentation of a specified set of shipping documents (bill of lading, commercial invoice, packing list, certificate of origin, and so on). The letter of credit may be "confirmed" by a bank in the seller's country, which means that bank undertakes to pay the seller on presentation of complying documents, regardless of whether the issuing bank actually pays.

The confirmed irrevocable L/C provides the seller with a payment obligation from a bank in their own jurisdiction — subject only to the requirement that the shipping documents strictly comply with the terms of the credit. That last condition is critical: the documents must conform exactly to the L/C requirements. A bill of lading that is one day outside the permitted shipment date, or a commercial invoice that describes the goods in slightly different terms to the credit, can give the bank grounds to refuse payment. Work with your freight forwarder and your bank closely to ensure that every document is prepared in exact conformity with the credit terms before you ship.

Letters of credit have costs — bank fees, amendment fees, negotiation fees — and they are administratively complex. For smaller transactions, or in established trading relationships where trust has been built over time, simpler payment mechanisms may be appropriate. But for significant transactions with new counterparts, the L/C is worth its cost.

Documentary Collections

A documentary collection is a simpler and less expensive mechanism than an L/C, but it provides less security. In a documentary collection, the seller ships the goods and sends the shipping documents to their bank, which forwards them to the buyer's bank with instructions to release them only against payment (Documents against Payment, or D/P) or against the buyer's acceptance of a bill of exchange (Documents against Acceptance, or D/A).

The key difference from an L/C is that the bank does not itself guarantee payment. It merely acts as a collecting agent. If the buyer refuses to pay or accept, the bank has no obligation to you — and you are left with your goods in the buyer's country, potentially stranded at the port, with no clear path to recovering them.

Documentary collections are appropriate in trading relationships where you have some basis for trusting the buyer, the buyer's country is politically and financially stable, and the goods can be easily redirected or resold if the buyer defaults. They are not appropriate for first transactions with unknown counterparts, or for transactions in politically or financially unstable markets.

Open Account Trading

Open account trading — where you ship the goods and invoice the buyer, who pays within a specified period — is the most common method of payment in domestic trade and in established international trading relationships. It is also the riskiest for the seller in a new or uncertain relationship, because it places the entire burden of credit risk on the seller.

Open account trading is appropriate where the buyer is well-known, financially strong, and operating in a stable legal environment where the seller has practical means of recovery if the buyer defaults. It is often used in established relationships where the parties have been trading successfully for years. It is rarely appropriate for first transactions in unfamiliar markets.

Export Credit Insurance

Export Finance Australia (EFA, formerly EFIC) provides export credit insurance and financial support for Australian exporters, covering risks that commercial insurance does not typically address — including political risk, buyer insolvency, and default on payment. The insurance is available to businesses of varying sizes, and it can make possible transactions that would otherwise be too risky to undertake.

EFA also provides guarantees that help exporters access finance from commercial banks, and direct loans for larger export transactions. For exporters entering new or uncertain markets, the EFA support suite is worth investigating early in the planning process. Their website at efa.com.au provides detailed information on available products.

Currency Risk

If your contract is denominated in a currency other than Australian dollars, you are exposed to exchange rate movements between the time the contract is signed and the time payment is received. A movement of even a few percentage points in the exchange rate can materially affect your profit margin on a transaction.

The standard tools for managing currency risk are forward foreign exchange contracts — arrangements with your bank to buy or sell a specified amount of foreign currency at a specified rate on a specified future date — and currency options, which give you the right but not the obligation to transact at a specified rate. Both instruments have costs, but those costs are predictable, unlike the cost of leaving currency risk unmanaged.

Talk to your bank's international trade desk early about currency risk management. It is one of the areas where the banks' expertise and infrastructure can genuinely save you money, and it is frequently overlooked by traders who are focused on the operational side of the transaction.

PART FOUR

Getting Your Goods There

Freight, shipping, insurance, customs, and the supply chain

CHAPTER 9

The Supply Chain: An Overview

The supply chain is the sequence of steps, parties, and processes that gets your goods from the seller's premises to the buyer's premises. In a domestic transaction, the supply chain may consist of a truck and a driver. In an international transaction, it typically involves a dozen or more parties, three or four different modes of transport, multiple border crossings, and a documentation trail that must be maintained with precision from start to finish.

This chapter provides a map of the supply chain. Subsequent chapters address each element in detail.

The Participants

The freight forwarder is your primary logistics manager. A good freight forwarder will manage every element of the physical supply chain on your behalf: booking the cargo space, arranging the inland transport to and from the port, preparing the shipping documentation, liaising with the customs broker, and tracking the shipment at every stage. Choose your freight forwarder carefully. They are not all equal, and the gap between a good one and a mediocre one can be the difference between a cargo that arrives on time, in good condition, with all the documentation in order, and a cargo that doesn't.

The customs broker handles the regulatory compliance side of border crossings. They prepare and lodge the customs declarations, calculate the duties and taxes payable, liaise with quarantine authorities, and manage any compliance issues that arise. Like freight forwarders, customs brokers vary in quality. In complex regulatory environments — and Australia's is not simple — a good customs broker is invaluable.

The inspection agency provides pre-shipment and port inspection services. As I discussed in Chapter 6, the pre-shipment inspection is one of the most cost-effective risk management tools available to importers. Companies like SGS, Bureau Veritas, and Intertek operate globally and can provide inspection certificates that satisfy both your requirements and any documentary credit conditions.

The insurer provides marine cargo insurance, covering loss or damage to the goods during transit. Marine insurance is addressed in detail in Chapter 11.

The carrier is the company that physically moves the goods — the shipping line, the airline, the trucking company, the rail operator. The carrier issues the key transport document (bill of lading for sea freight, air waybill for air freight) that functions as both a receipt for the goods and, in the case of a bill of lading, a document of title.

The Bill of Lading

The bill of lading deserves special attention, because it is the most important document in sea freight logistics. In its traditional form, it is three things simultaneously: a receipt from the carrier acknowledging that the goods have been received for shipment; evidence of the contract of carriage between the shipper and the carrier; and a document of title — meaning that whoever holds the original bill of lading is entitled to take delivery of the goods.

That third function — the negotiability of the bill of lading — is what makes the documentary credit system work. The exporter ships the goods and obtains a bill of lading from the carrier. They present the bill, with the other required documents, to their bank. The bank pays the exporter and forwards the documents to the buyer's bank. The buyer's bank releases the documents to the buyer. The buyer presents the original bill of lading at the destination port and takes delivery of the goods. At each step, the bill travels with the payment obligation, and neither can be separated from the other without the transaction breaking down.

This system is centuries old, and it is the subject of an entire volume in this series — Book Two: Bills of Lading in Shipping Law: An Australian Perspective. I strongly recommend that volume to any trader who is moving significant cargo by sea, and to any practitioner advising on sea freight transactions.

Air Freight vs Sea Freight

The choice between air freight and sea freight is driven by three factors: the time sensitivity of the cargo, the cost of the goods relative to the freight cost, and any specific requirements of the cargo itself.

Sea freight is slower and cheaper. Transit times from Australia to Asia run from a few days to a few weeks depending on the destination; to Europe, allow four to six weeks. Sea freight is cost-effective for high-volume, low-value goods, or goods where the transit time does not matter commercially.

Air freight is faster and more expensive — typically three to ten times the cost of sea freight by weight. It is appropriate for time-sensitive goods (perishables, fashion, electronics, pharmaceutical products), high-value goods where the freight cost is a small proportion of the total value, and emergency shipments where speed outweighs cost.

Intermodal arrangements — combining air and sea, or sea and rail — can offer a compromise between speed and cost for certain routes. Your freight forwarder can advise on the options for your specific cargo and destination.

Choosing a Freight Forwarder

A good freight forwarder has a comprehensive network — owned offices or established agency relationships in the markets you are trading in. They offer transparency and tracking, so you know where your cargo is at every stage. They have specialist capability for your type of cargo: perishables, hazardous goods, oversized freight, and temperature-sensitive shipments all require specific knowledge and equipment. They have a track record and references you can verify. And they have a realistic pricing structure — not necessarily the cheapest, but one that reflects the quality of service they actually provide.

Cheap freight has hidden costs. A forwarder who holds cargo until they have a full container load, saving themselves the cost of a partial shipment, can leave your customer waiting and your business relationship strained. A forwarder without comprehensive tracking capability leaves you unable to answer customer inquiries about delivery. A forwarder whose depot management is poor leaves your cargo more vulnerable to damage and loss. The cost differential between a good forwarder and a cheap one is almost always smaller than the cost differential between a smooth transaction and a problematic one.

CHAPTER 10
Insurance: Don't Leave Home Without It

Marine cargo insurance is one of the oldest and most sophisticated branches of the insurance industry. The first marine insurance policies were written in Italy in the twelfth century. By the sixteenth century, the practice had reached Northern Europe. The Lloyd's of London market — which still dominates marine insurance globally — traces its origins to Edward Lloyd's coffee house in the City of London in the seventeenth century, where shipowners, merchants, and insurers gathered to exchange information and do business.

I mention this history because it matters. Marine insurance is not a generic product that can be purchased off the shelf and assumed to cover everything. It is a highly specialised field, with its own conventions, exclusions, and interpretive principles, and the gap between the coverage you think you have and the coverage you actually have can be very expensive to discover.

To Insure or Not to Insure

Let me answer this question directly: insure. Always.

The question is not whether to insure your international cargo, but how to insure it correctly.

The cost of marine cargo insurance is typically a fraction of a percent of the cargo value. The cost of an uninsured loss — or an insured loss that is rejected on a technicality because the coverage was not appropriate — is the full value of the cargo, plus the freight, plus the demurrage, plus any third-party liability, plus the cost of disposal if the cargo cannot be landed.

I have sat across the desk from traders who were not insured when they should have been. It is a very uncomfortable conversation. Do not be in that position.

The Institute Cargo Clauses

Marine cargo insurance in most markets is written on the basis of the Institute Cargo Clauses, developed by the Institute of London Underwriters and revised over the years. The three main sets are Institute Cargo Clauses (A), (B), and (C), which provide progressively broader coverage in that order, with (A) being the most comprehensive.

Clause (A) covers all risks of loss or damage except a defined list of exclusions, including inherent vice (the tendency of the cargo itself to deteriorate), deliberate misconduct of the assured, and certain war and strike risks (which can be added by separate clauses). Clause (C) covers only specified risks — fire, explosion, stranding, collision, and a few others — and is the narrowest standard form available.

For most general cargo, Clause (A) cover is appropriate. For specific cargo types — bulk liquids, refrigerated goods, livestock, fine art, hazardous materials — specialist clauses apply, and the choice of coverage should be made in consultation with a specialist broker who knows your cargo type.

The Duty of Utmost Good Faith

Marine insurance policies, like all insurance contracts, are governed by the principle of utmost good faith (uberrima fides). This means that you, as the insured, must disclose to the insurer all material facts that could affect the insurer's decision to write the risk or the terms on which they will do so. Failure to disclose material facts can entitle the insurer to avoid the policy and refuse to pay claims.

Material facts include: the nature and value of the cargo; the packaging; the route; the mode of transport; any known defects or vulnerabilities; the terms of the underlying commercial contract; and any previous claims on similar cargo. When in doubt, disclose. The insurer can then make an informed decision about the risk, and you can be confident that the coverage you have purchased is valid.

War, Terrorism, and Piracy Risks

Standard Institute Cargo Clauses exclude war, terrorism, and piracy risks. These can be added by separate clauses — the Institute War Clauses and the Institute Strikes Clauses — at an additional premium. Whether you need them depends on your route and cargo.

Some shipping routes pass through areas of elevated piracy or conflict risk, and the additional premium for war and piracy cover on those routes is not large relative to the protection it provides. Check with your broker whether your intended route falls within any current advisory areas, and include war and strikes cover if there is any realistic possibility of exposure.

Finding a Good Broker

The most important step in managing your insurance correctly is finding a broker who specialises in marine cargo and who genuinely understands your cargo type and your supply chain. Marine cargo insurance is not a commodity product, and a general insurance broker who also writes household and motor policies is not the right advisor for a complex international cargo.

A specialist marine broker will know which underwriters have appetite for your specific cargo type, which clauses are appropriate, and what conditions and exclusions to watch for.

They will help you prepare your disclosure correctly, advise you on how to value the cargo for insurance purposes (generally, the invoice value plus freight and insurance, plus a ten percent uplift for anticipated profit), and be your advocate in the event of a claim.

CHAPTER 11

Customs, Tariffs, and Getting Your Goods Through

Customs clearance is the regulatory checkpoint through which every international cargo must pass, and it is one of the most consistently underestimated elements of the supply chain. Traders who have mastered every other aspect of the transaction sometimes find themselves with goods stranded at the border because a classification is wrong, a permit is missing, or a document does not conform to the importing country's requirements.

"You don't know what you don't know."

The Harmonised System

Every product traded internationally is classified under the Harmonised System (HS), a globally standardised nomenclature maintained by the World Customs Organization. The HS code for your product determines the tariff rate it attracts, the documentation requirements that apply, and any restrictions or prohibitions that may affect its importation.

The HS code is a six-digit number. The first two digits identify the broad product chapter (for example, Chapter 10 covers cereals). The third and fourth digits narrow the classification to a heading. The fifth and sixth digits specify the subheading. Individual countries may add further digits to the code for their own statistical and tariff purposes — Australia uses an eight-digit code, the United States a ten-digit code.

Getting the HS code right is your responsibility as the trader, and the consequences of getting it wrong can be severe: non-compliance penalties, border delays, seizure of goods, denial of import privileges, and potential criminal liability for deliberate misdeclaration. Work with your customs broker to identify the correct code for your product, and do not assume that the code used in one country will be the same as the code used in another — classifications can vary, and the tariff consequences can be significant.

To illustrate the complexity: I was once involved in a tariff case in which one of the world's largest medical and pharmaceutical distributors imported operating theatre clothing — the disposable paper gowns, caps, and masks you see in hospitals.

Customs wanted them classified as fabric, attracting a substantial tariff. We argued for classification as paper goods, attracting a much lower rate. The case turned on the precise method of manufacture: we were able to prove that the gowns were made by laying down sheets of paper material and fusing them under water-jet pressure, rather than weaving or knitting fabric. The Court agreed they were paper goods. The case took months to prepare and required technical experts flown from the United States. The difference in tariff liability was substantial, potentially millions of dollars.

This is not an area for improvisation.

Import Duties and Taxes

When importing goods into Australia, the main charges you will encounter are customs import duty (calculated as a percentage of the customs value of the goods, typically ranging from zero to ten percent but varying significantly by product), Goods and Services Tax (GST, currently ten percent, applied to the customs value plus duty), and import processing charges levied by the Australian Border Force.

Australia has free trade agreements (FTAs) with a number of major trading partners, including China, Japan, South Korea, the United States, and the European Union, among others. Under an FTA, goods originating in the partner country may attract reduced or zero duty rates. Eligibility for preferential tariff treatment requires compliance with the rules of origin specified in the relevant agreement and the correct documentation to support the claim. Your customs broker can advise on which FTAs apply to your imports and what documentation is required.

Prohibited and Restricted Goods

Australia maintains lists of goods that are prohibited from import (narcotics, certain weapons, child exploitation material, and so on) and goods that are restricted — requiring specific permits or approvals before they can be cleared through customs (certain pharmaceuticals, biological materials, food products, weapons and firearms, and heritage-listed items, among others).

Check the Australian Border Force's list of prohibited and restricted goods at abf.gov.au before you commit to any import transaction. A cargo of goods that turns out to be restricted, without the necessary permit, can be seized at the border and the importer may be subject to significant penalties.

Quarantine and Biosecurity

Australia has some of the strictest biosecurity requirements in the world, reflecting the country's status as an island continent with unique and vulnerable ecosystems. The Department of Agriculture, Fisheries and Forestry administers biosecurity controls through the Australian Border Force at the border.

Goods of plant, animal, or mineral origin are subject to quarantine assessment and may require treatment (fumigation, heat treatment, irradiation) before they can be cleared. Certain goods may be prohibited entirely. If you are importing any goods with a biological component, get specific biosecurity advice before you place your order. A cargo that cannot clear quarantine is a very expensive problem.

Anti-Dumping

Anti-dumping measures are trade remedies applied when goods are imported at prices below their normal value in the country of origin, to the detriment of the domestic industry in the importing country. Australia administers anti-dumping measures through the Anti-Dumping Commission.

If you are importing goods that are also produced domestically in Australia, check whether anti-dumping or countervailing duties apply. These duties can be substantial, and they can change over time as new investigations are conducted or existing measures are varied. If you are an Australian manufacturer and you believe a foreign competitor is dumping goods in the Australian market, the Anti-Dumping Commission is the correct authority to contact.

CHAPTER 12

Packaging, Labelling, and Getting It Right at the Last Step

After all the commercial negotiation, the financial arrangements, the logistics planning, and the regulatory compliance work, the physical presentation of your product at the point of shipment is the last step before it leaves your control. It is also one of the steps most often managed carelessly, with results that range from annoying to catastrophic.

Why Packaging Matters

An international cargo travels far and is handled many times. From your factory or warehouse, it moves by road or rail to a port or airport. It is loaded into a container or onto a pallet, stacked with other cargo, and subjected to the vibration, shock, temperature variation, humidity, and pressure changes of a voyage that may last weeks. It is then unloaded, inspected, transported to a warehouse, and finally delivered to the end customer.

At every one of those stages, inadequate packaging can cause damage. And when the goods arrive damaged, the consequence is not just the cost of the damage itself. It is the cost of arranging replacements, the delay in getting good product to the customer, the loss of trust that comes from a bad first impression, and the prospect of a complex insurance claim that may or may not succeed.

Packaging your goods correctly is not an afterthought. It is a commercial requirement.

Principles of Good Packaging

The general principle is straightforward: the goods should be packaged in a way that protects them against all foreseeable hazards of the intended journey. What those hazards are depends on the cargo, the route, the mode of transport, and the climate conditions the cargo will encounter.

For fragile goods, this means adequate cushioning and void fill to absorb impact, and a container that is rigid enough to withstand the compressive load of cargo stacked above it. For moisture-sensitive goods, it means moisture-resistant outer packaging and desiccant materials inside. For temperature-sensitive goods, it means appropriate thermal insulation, and, for perishables, a refrigerated container managed at the correct temperature throughout the voyage. For goods that are vulnerable to compression, it means packaging that distributes the load across the surface rather than concentrating it at the weakest points.

Labelling Requirements

At a minimum, imported goods must be clearly and accurately labelled with the country of manufacture and origin, a true description of the goods, sender and recipient addresses, and any required handling instructions. In some markets, labelling requirements are significantly more demanding — mandatory language requirements, specific ingredient disclosures, nutritional information formats, safety warnings, and so on. These requirements vary by product and by destination market.

Check the labelling requirements of your destination market before you design your packaging. Redesigning labels after production is expensive. Discovering at the border that your labelling does not comply is worse.

Packaging for the Container

If you are shipping in a full container load (FCL), the entire container is your cargo space. The container should be loaded so that the cargo is stable, evenly distributed across the floor, and secured against movement during transit. Cargo that shifts during a voyage can be damaged by impact and can compromise the structural integrity of the container.

If you are shipping a less-than-container-load (LCL), your cargo will be consolidated with other shippers' cargo in a container.

This means your goods will be handled and positioned by people who do not know your cargo, and they will travel alongside goods of different sizes, weights, and handling requirements. Robust outer packaging is essential, and clear handling instructions should be marked conspicuously on the exterior.

PART FIVE

On the Ground

Visiting your market, building relationships, and travelling safely

CHAPTER 13

The Business Trip: Preparing to Go

No amount of desk research substitutes for being there. The conversations you have face to face with a potential buyer, supplier, or partner reveal things that email and video calls cannot. The walk through a market, a factory, or a retail district gives you information that no database contains. The relationship that begins with a meal and a handshake often proves more durable than one built entirely through digital channels.

That said, a business trip to a foreign market is an investment of time and money that needs to be planned carefully to justify its cost. This chapter covers the preparation. Chapter 14 covers the travel itself.

Setting Your Objectives

Before you book anything, write down what you want to achieve from this trip. Not in vague terms — "build relationships" or "explore the market" — but in specific, measurable terms. By the end of this trip, I will have: met at least three potential buyers and assessed their suitability; visited the production facility of my target supplier and verified their capability; confirmed the logistics chain for the intended route; and obtained names and contact details for a customs broker and freight forwarder in the target city.

With clear objectives, you can plan your schedule, allocate your time, and evaluate the trip's success when you return. Without them, a trip can consume two weeks and a significant budget while producing little that is actionable.

Pre-Trip Research

By the time you book your flights, you should already have: a list of pre-arranged meetings, preferably made through warm introductions from Austrade, your bank, your industry association, or a mutual contact; a briefing document on each counterpart you will be meeting, drawn from online research and any information your contacts have provided; a clear understanding of the cultural norms governing business meetings in the target country — dress codes, gift-giving expectations, negotiating conventions, the role of hierarchy in decision-making, and the appropriate pace of relationship-building; and an understanding of the practical logistics — how to get from the airport to your hotel, which transport options are reliable, what the business hours are, and what the current political and security situation is.

For Australian travellers, the Department of Foreign Affairs and Trade's Smartraveller service (smartraveller.gov.au) provides up-to-date travel advisories, entry requirements, and consular information for every country. Register your trip before you leave, so that consular staff know you are in the country and can assist if something goes wrong.

Meetings: Preparation and Conduct

Prepare for each meeting as you would for a client presentation at home: know who you are meeting, what they do, what they need, and what you want from the interaction. Have your materials ready — product samples, capability statements, pricing schedules, translated into the local language where relevant. Have business cards printed in both English and the local language. Bring more cards than you think you will need.

In many Asian business cultures, the exchange of business cards is a formal ritual and the card should be treated with respect — received with both hands, read carefully before putting away. Offering a card that has been casually scribbled on, or putting a received card in your back pocket, is a genuine discourtesy in these contexts. Research the specific conventions of the country you are visiting.

Allow more time between meetings than you think you need. In busy cities, traffic is often severe and unpredictable. Arriving late to a meeting in a culture that places high value on punctuality makes a bad first impression that is difficult to repair.

Getting Ready for Each Day

At the end of each day, update your notes while the conversations are fresh. Note what was said, what was agreed, what was unclear, and what follow-up actions are required from each side. Upload your notes to cloud storage so they are accessible from home. Brief your colleagues back in Australia on any commercially significant developments while the information is current. Prepare your materials for the next day's meetings.

If you are travelling with colleagues, hold a brief end-of-day debrief. Ensure everyone has the same understanding of what occurred and what is expected next. Misunderstandings within your own team, communicated to counterparts through inconsistent messages, can undermine the trust you are trying to build.

CHAPTER 14

Travel Tips: Practical Wisdom for the Road

I have flown around the world more times than I can accurately count, and accumulated a collection of hard-won practical lessons that no travel guide quite captures. Here is the distilled version, in plain language.

The most important principle of business travel is this: keep it simple. Every unnecessary complication — the extra bag, the ambitious itinerary, the assumption that things will work as they do at home — is a source of friction that costs you energy you need for business.

Before You Leave

Check your passport validity. Many countries require at least six months of remaining validity beyond your intended departure date. Some require a minimum number of blank pages. Check both requirements for every country on your itinerary.

Register with Smartraveller at smartraveller.gov.au and leave a complete copy of your itinerary with someone at home, including hotel addresses and emergency contact numbers. If something goes wrong, this is what allows consular staff to find you.

Arrange your visas well in advance. Processing times for some countries can be weeks, and the consequences of arriving at a border without the correct visa are severe. For frequently visited markets, investigate whether a business visa or multi-entry arrangement is available.

Get vaccinated for any destination that requires it, and consult a travel medicine clinic about recommended preventive measures. The clinic visit costs less than a day's hotel room. Falling ill in a foreign country costs far more.

Arrange travel insurance that covers medical evacuation, not just treatment. In some countries, the quality of available medical care is such that evacuation to a major regional centre or back to Australia may be the only responsible option in a serious medical emergency. This is not covered by standard travel insurance policies.

Packing

Pack light. If you are on a trip of less than a week, one carry-on bag is sufficient for most business travel. The time saved not checking luggage, and the anxiety avoided by not having bags lost, is worth the minor constraint of packing efficiently.

Keep your essentials in your carry-on: passport, medications, laptop, chargers, and a change of clothes for the first day. If your checked baggage is delayed, these things keep you functional.

Carry photocopies of your passport photo page, your travel insurance policy, and your credit cards. Store these separately from the originals, and email copies to yourself. If your wallet is lost or stolen, this is what makes recovery possible. I once lost my wallet in Riga, Latvia. Without the photo ID and the ability to provide my card details over the phone, the recovery process would have been far more difficult and time-consuming.

Money and Currency

Carry some local currency from the moment you land. Exchanging a modest amount — the equivalent of a couple of hundred Australian dollars — before you leave allows you to cover immediate expenses (transport from the airport, tips, small purchases) without having to find a currency exchange at an unfamiliar airport while tired from a long flight.

Most banks offer multi-currency travel cards that allow you to load funds in the currency of your destination at a known exchange rate. These are significantly more economical than using your standard credit card for foreign currency transactions. Notify your bank and credit card company of your travel plans before you leave, or you risk having your card blocked as a fraud precaution when it appears in an unexpected location.

Health and Hygiene

In countries where the tap water is not reliably safe to drink — which includes most of the developing world and some parts of the developed world — drink only bottled water from sealed containers that you have personally opened. Avoid ice cubes in drinks unless you are confident of their origin. Be cautious about salads and unpeeled raw fruit, which may have been washed in tap water. Carry oral rehydration sachets, and take traveller's diarrhoea medication as a precaution.

Get enough sleep. Business travel is physically and cognitively demanding, and decision-making under pressure in an unfamiliar environment is significantly more difficult when you are fatigued. Adjust your sleep schedule to the local time zone as quickly as possible upon arrival. Stay hydrated, particularly on long flights where the cabin air is very dry.

Security

In most of the world, most of the time, the risks to a prudent business traveller are manageable. Use common sense. In unfamiliar areas, especially at night, stay alert to your surroundings. Keep valuable items — laptop, passport, wallet — secured rather than left in plain view. Avoid displaying expensive watches, jewellery, or electronics in environments where they attract attention.

On public wi-fi networks, use a VPN to protect your data. Avoid accessing banking systems or confidential business information on unsecured public networks. In countries where the government monitors internet traffic, be aware that what you communicate digitally may not be private.

And finally: keep an open mind. The purpose of going to a foreign market is to understand it, not to confirm your existing assumptions about it. The traveller who is genuinely curious, genuinely respectful, and genuinely willing to listen will learn things that the traveller who merely executes a pre-planned agenda never will. Those things may be the most commercially valuable things you bring home.

PART SIX

Reference

Glossary, abbreviations, and container specifications

CHAPTER 15

Freight Glossary and Abbreviations

The freight industry is built on abbreviations. This chapter provides a practical reference for the terms you will encounter most frequently in air and sea freight.

Documents

AWB / HAWB — Air Waybill / House Air Waybill. A waybill is a document issued by a carrier or forwarder giving details and instructions relating to a shipment. Unlike a bill of lading, an air waybill is not a document of title.

B/L or BOL — Bill of Lading. A document issued by the carrier to the shipper as both a receipt for the goods and evidence of the contract of carriage. A negotiable bill of lading is also a document of title. See Chapter 9 and Book Two in this series for detailed treatment.

L/C — Letter of Credit. A document issued by a bank guaranteeing payment to the seller upon presentation of specified documents. See Chapter 8.

MSDS — Material Safety Data Sheet. Provides handling procedures for dangerous goods. Mandatory for goods classified as dangerous.

People and Places

CNOR / CNEE — Consignor / Consignee. The sender and receiver of the goods.

ETD / ETA — Estimated Time of Departure / Estimated Time of Arrival.

ATD / ATA — Actual Time of Departure / Actual Time of Arrival.

POL / POD — Port of Loading / Port of Discharge.

NVOCC — Non-Vessel Operating Common Carrier. Acts as a shipping line but does not own ships.

CFS — Container Freight Station. A cargo handling depot where LCL shipments are consolidated and deconsolidated.

Container and Cargo Types

FCL — Full Container Load. The shipper uses the entire container.

LCL — Less than Container Load. The shipper's cargo shares a container with other shippers' cargo. Minimum shipment size is typically one cubic metre.

TEU — Twenty-foot Equivalent Unit. The standard unit of container capacity, equivalent to one twenty-foot container.

FEU — Forty-foot Equivalent Unit.

HC — High Cube container. One foot taller than a standard container, allowing greater cubic capacity.

RF / Reefer — Refrigerated Container. For temperature-sensitive cargo.

OT — Open Top Container. For cargo that cannot be loaded through the container doors.

FR — Flat Rack. For oversized or out-of-gauge cargo.

OOG — Out of Gauge. Cargo that exceeds the standard dimensions of a shipping container.

RoRo — Roll on Roll Off. Cargo that can be driven or towed onto a vessel.

B/B, B/Bulk — Break-Bulk. Large cargo loaded directly onto the vessel, not in a container.

Freight Charges and Surcharges

BAF — Bunker Adjustment Factor. A surcharge reflecting fuel costs for the vessel.

CAF — Currency Adjustment Factor. A surcharge reflecting currency fluctuation.

GRI — General Rate Increase. A general increase in ocean freight rates on a particular trade route.

FAF — Fuel Adjustment Factor. Applied to road transport or airfreight.

Dimensions and Measurement

CBM / M^3 — Cubic Metres. Calculated as Height x Width x Length. The standard unit of volume in freight pricing.

W/M — Weight or Measure. Billing based on whichever of weight or volume produces the higher freight charge. Commonly applied in LCL sea freight.

KG — Kilograms.

CHAPTER 16

Shipping Container Specifications

Shipping containers come in a range of standard sizes and specialised types. The specifications below are drawn from industry standards; note that exact dimensions can vary slightly by manufacturer, and load regulations may restrict operation to less than the stated maximum weights.

When choosing a container type, consult your freight forwarder. The right container for your cargo depends on its dimensions, weight, temperature requirements, and the route it will travel. Do not assume that the container offered by the shipping line is necessarily the most appropriate for your cargo.

Standard Containers

20-foot Standard (TEU): External length 6.058m; external width 2.438m; external height 2.591m. Internal volume approximately 33 cubic metres. Maximum payload approximately 21,700kg.

40-foot Standard (FEU): External length 12.192m; external width 2.438m; external height 2.591m. Internal volume approximately 67 cubic metres. Maximum payload approximately 26,680kg.

40-foot High Cube: Same footprint as the 40-foot standard, but one foot taller at 2.896m external height. Internal volume approximately 76 cubic metres. Popular for lightweight, voluminous cargo.

Specialised Containers

Refrigerated (Reefer) Containers: Available in 20-foot and 40-foot sizes. Maintain a controlled temperature throughout the voyage. Required for fresh produce, frozen goods, pharmaceuticals, and other temperature-sensitive cargo. Require power at the terminal and on the vessel.

Open Top Containers: Standard footprint, but with a removable roof to allow loading by crane. Used for cargo that cannot be loaded through the container doors due to height or configuration. Subject to availability and additional surcharges.

Flat Rack Containers: For oversized or out-of-gauge cargo. The sides fold down, allowing loading from the side or above. Additional surcharges apply for out-of-gauge cargo.

A Note on Container Condition

As I discussed in Chapter 2, container condition is a real and underestimated risk in Australian export trade. The longest routes tend to receive the oldest containers. A small defect in a container — a compromised seal, a small hole in the roof panel, a corroded corner casting — can allow water ingress over a long voyage, with potentially devastating consequences for moisture-sensitive cargo. Always inspect the container before loading, and document any defects. If the container is not in sound condition, request a replacement.

APPENDIX 1

Drafting International Contracts: Practical Tips

This appendix sets out the key principles of good international contract drafting. It is intended as a framework for discussion with your lawyer, not as a substitute for legal advice.

1. Identify the parties precisely. Full legal names, registration numbers, registered addresses, and the jurisdiction of incorporation. Errors in party identification can create ambiguity about who is bound by the contract.

2. Describe the goods or services with precision. Reference to approved samples, specifications, or standards documents is preferable to reliance on general descriptions. “Goods of merchantable quality” is not a specification.

3. State the price, currency, and payment terms unambiguously. Include the Incoterm that applies and the named place, as this determines how the price is structured (cost only, or cost plus freight, or cost plus freight plus insurance).

4. Specify the governing law clearly. The governing law clause is not a formality. It determines how ambiguous clauses will be interpreted and what remedies are available if the contract is breached.

5. Address dispute resolution thoughtfully. For most international commercial contracts, arbitration is preferable to litigation, because arbitral awards are more readily enforceable across borders. Specify the arbitration rules, the seat of arbitration, and the language of proceedings. Take advice on whether the chosen seat will give you practical enforcement against your counterpart's assets.

6. Include a force majeure clause, but draft it carefully. Overly broad force majeure clauses can allow counterparts to avoid obligations that they could perform with reasonable effort. Define the qualifying events specifically.

7. Address intellectual property clearly. Who owns what is created or shared during performance of the contract? What can each party do with the other's IP during and after the contract?

8. Use plain English. The goal is precision, not complexity. A contract that both parties can read and understand is less likely to give rise to disputes than one that requires a lawyer to interpret every clause.

9. Have both parties' lawyers review the final document. The investment is small relative to the value of most international commercial contracts.

10. Keep signed originals in a secure place. In a dispute, the original signed contract is your primary evidence of what was agreed.

APPENDIX 2

International Etiquette: Thirty Principles for Business Across Cultures

This appendix provides a summary of the key cultural principles that most commonly affect international business relationships. It is necessarily general: the diversity of business cultures across the world is too great to address comprehensively in a short reference. The specific norms of any target market should be researched carefully before your first visit. The resource I recommend most highly is globalnegotiator.com, which provides detailed cultural guidance for business in most countries.

The fundamental principle: assume nothing. The cultural assumptions that feel like common sense in Australia — about directness, punctuality, informality, eye contact, the role of humour, and the pace of decision-making — are not universal. What reads as confidence in one culture reads as arrogance in another. What reads as respect in one culture reads as weakness in another.

Below are thirty general principles that apply, with local variations, across most international business contexts.

1. Research the specific cultural norms of your target country before you travel. General principles are a starting point, not a destination.

2. Learn a few words of the local language — at minimum, "please," "thank you," and "I'm sorry." The effort is noticed and appreciated.

3. Dress conservatively for initial meetings. You can always become more casual as the relationship develops. You cannot undo a bad first impression.

4. Be punctual. In most business cultures, even those with a more relaxed attitude to time than Australia, being on time for a business meeting is a sign of respect.

5. Do not assume that the senior person in the room is the most vocal. In many Asian business cultures, the decision-maker is often the quiet person at the head of the table.

6. Treat business cards with respect. Receive them with both hands, read them before putting them away, and do not write on them.

7. Do not rush. In many cultures, the process of building relationship and establishing trust is an essential precondition to business, not a formality to be dispensed with.

8. Do not assume that agreement in a meeting means agreement on a contract. In some cultures, "yes" in a meeting means "I hear you," not "I agree."

9. Do not send your most junior representative to an initial meeting. In hierarchy-conscious cultures, this is disrespectful.

10. Avoid direct criticism or contradiction in a meeting. Many cultures have strong norms around face-saving, and a direct statement that someone is wrong can destroy a relationship.

11. China: Address the most senior person first. Wait for them to be seated before you sit. Do not use first names unless invited to do so.

12. Japan: Silence is not uncomfortable. Do not fill it. The Japanese use silence to indicate thought, not discomfort.

13. Middle East: Relationships are paramount. Do not expect to conduct significant business on a first visit. The relationship must be established before business is done.

14. India: Business meetings often involve discussion of matters unrelated to business. This is relationship-building, not distraction.

15. Brazil: Physical contact is more common in greeting than in most Western cultures. Brazilians do not identify as "Latin American" or "Hispanic" — they are Brazilian.

16. Germany: Formality and precision are valued. Do not use first names until invited. Be specific in your proposals — vague generalisations are not persuasive.

17. France: Criticising French products, food, or culture is a shortcut to a difficult relationship. French counterparts expect intellectual engagement, not just commercial propositions.

18. Russia: Building personal rapport is important before business can be done. Social occasions, including shared meals and vodka, are part of the process, not peripheral to it.

19. South Korea: Age and seniority are deeply respected. Pour drinks for others before pouring your own.

20. Australia: Our directness and informality, which feel like honesty and friendliness at home, can read as rudeness or lack of seriousness in other cultures. Be conscious of this.

21. Always bring sufficient business cards, printed in English and, if possible, the local language.

22. Gifts are appropriate in many business cultures and inappropriate in others. Research the local conventions before you pack anything.

23. Do not discuss money, salaries, or personal finances unless invited to do so. In many cultures, this is deeply private.

24. Religious and political sensitivities vary enormously. When in doubt, do not comment.

25. Keep your sense of humour, but recognise that jokes do not always translate. What is funny in English may be meaningless or offensive in translation.

26. Observe how your hosts interact with each other. The hierarchy, the communication style, and the decision-making process will be visible if you pay attention.

27. Follow your host's lead on meals, drinks, and social occasions. You do not have to drink alcohol, but you should acknowledge the hospitality.

28. Follow up after meetings promptly. A brief email confirming what was discussed and agreed demonstrates reliability and keeps the relationship active.

29. Never speak disparagingly about your competitors in front of a potential client. In many cultures, this reflects badly on you, not on the competitor.

30. Keep an open mind. The cultural differences that initially seem strange often reflect deeply considered values. The traveller who is genuinely curious, and genuinely respectful, will always do better than the one who is merely tolerant.

APPENDIX 3

China Contracts: Make Them Enforceable or Don't Bother

The following is reproduced and adapted from "China Contracts: Make Them Enforceable or Don't Bother" by Steve Dickinson, published on the China Law Blog (chinalawblog.com) on 18 August 2015, with the permission of the author. The China Law Blog is the leading English-language resource for analysis of Chinese commercial and business law. All adaptations are the author's own. Readers are encouraged to consult the original article and the China Law Blog for ongoing developments in Chinese commercial law.

Every businessperson who enters into a contract with a Chinese company needs to consider a fundamental question: how will the contract be enforced if a dispute arises? The answer to that question should drive how the contract is structured from the outset.

The Basic Requirements for Enforceability

For a contract to be practically enforceable against a Chinese company in a Chinese court, it typically needs to satisfy four conditions.

First, there must be a written contract, executed by both parties in accordance with Chinese legal requirements. Chinese courts will not assemble a contract from a collection of purchase orders, emails, and invoices, as courts in common law jurisdictions might.

Second, the contract should be governed by Chinese law. While it is legally permissible to specify a foreign governing law, doing so makes the contract nearly impossible to use in a Chinese court, because the court must then receive expert evidence on the content of the foreign law — an expensive, time-consuming, and unreliable process.

Third, the governing language of the contract should be Chinese. Contracts in foreign languages must be translated by a court-appointed translator, whose translation may be inaccurate and which the defendant will in any event dispute, adding delay and uncertainty.

Fourth, the dispute resolution clause should specify a Chinese court with jurisdiction over the defendant — normally the court in the district where the defendant has its principal place of business. A Beijing arbitration clause against a defendant based in a provincial city may be of limited practical use, because Chinese courts in one district are often reluctant to enforce orders from courts in another.

This does not mean that arbitration is always wrong for China contracts. China has experienced and well-regarded arbitration panels with extensive Sino-foreign dispute experience. For some types of dispute, and for some types of relief, arbitration may be appropriate. But the default assumption that an ICC clause in English will be enforceable in China is incorrect, and acting on that assumption can be very expensive.

The practical implication is straightforward: if you are entering into a significant commercial contract with a Chinese counterpart, engage a lawyer who practices Chinese law and has experience with Chinese courts or arbitration panels. Do not simply take your domestic contract and add a Chinese counterpart's name to it. The thirty pages of beautifully drafted English contract that my client brought to me were, from the perspective of enforcement in China, substantially worthless. Do not make the same mistake.

For the full article by Steve Dickinson, and ongoing analysis of Chinese commercial law developments, the China Law Blog (chinalawblog.com) is the best English-language resource available.

APPENDIX 4

International Contract Templates: Where to Find Them

There is a temptation, particularly for traders who are careful with their money, to draft their own international commercial contracts using templates found online. I understand the temptation. I strongly caution against it.

International commercial contracts address genuinely complex legal situations. The governing law clause, the dispute resolution provision, the force majeure clause, the IP ownership provisions, and the liability limitations all interact with each other in ways that are not obvious from the face of the document. A clause that is appropriate in one jurisdiction may be void or unenforceable in another. A template designed for one type of transaction may produce unexpected results when applied to a different one.

That said, template contracts can be valuable — as a starting point for understanding the structure and scope of a properly drafted international contract, and as a reference document that your lawyer can work from and adapt to your specific circumstances. The key is to treat them as a framework, not a finished product.

The International Trade Centre Model Contracts

The International Trade Centre (a joint agency of the United Nations and the World Trade Organization) has published a suite of model contracts for small and medium enterprises, developed in collaboration with international legal experts. These contracts are available free of charge at intracen.org/itc/exporters/model-contracts/ and represent a well-considered starting point.

The suite includes model contracts for: the international sale of goods; the long-term supply of goods; the international distribution of goods; commercial agency; joint venture; manufacture; and the supply of services. Each is available in English, French, Spanish, and Portuguese.

These contracts are frameworks, not finished products. Each one will require adaptation to the specific commercial circumstances and the specific legal requirements of the jurisdictions involved. Always have any contract reviewed by qualified lawyers at both ends of the transaction before signing.

Commercial Contract Publishers

For more specialised contract forms, two resources are worth noting. Globalnegotiator.com provides a range of commercial contract templates developed for international trade, as well as cultural guidance and negotiation resources. Internationalcontracts.net offers similar resources with a focus on practical commercial documentation.

Both sites charge for their contract forms. The cost is modest relative to the value of a well-drafted contract, but remember that the template is still a starting point, not a substitute for legal advice.

APPENDIX 5

Incoterms 2020: Quick Reference

Incoterms (International Commercial Terms) are standardised trade terms published by the International Chamber of Commerce that define the obligations, costs, and risks of buyer and seller in international trade. The current edition is Incoterms 2020. They are incorporated by reference into sales contracts worldwide.

Incoterms do not address: the transfer of ownership (title) to the goods; the price or payment terms; the governing law of the contract; or the consequences of breach. They address only the physical delivery of the goods and the allocation of transport costs and risk between the parties.

Rules for Any Mode of Transport

EXW — Ex Works (named place): The seller makes the goods available at their premises. The buyer bears all costs and risks from that point. Maximum obligation on buyer, minimum on seller. Not recommended where the buyer is unfamiliar with the seller's country's export requirements.

FCA — Free Carrier (named place): The seller delivers the goods, cleared for export, to a carrier nominated by the buyer.

Risk passes to the buyer at the named place. Recommended for containerised freight.

CPT — Carriage Paid To (named destination): The seller pays freight to the named destination, but risk passes to the buyer when the goods are handed to the first carrier in the seller's country. Recommended for containerised freight; only use with a letter of credit.

CIP — Carriage and Insurance Paid To (named destination): As CPT, but the seller also arranges insurance to the named destination. Recommended for containerised freight; only use with a letter of credit.

DAP — Delivered at Place (named destination): The seller delivers to the named destination, ready for unloading. All costs and risks up to that point are the seller's, except import duties. Maximum obligation on seller; only appropriate where seller has reliable logistics capability in the buyer's country.

DPU — Delivered at Place Unloaded (named destination): As DAP, but the seller is also responsible for unloading at the named destination. New in Incoterms 2020.

DDP — Delivered Duty Paid (named destination): The seller bears all costs and risks including import duties. Maximum obligation on seller; only use where seller has thorough knowledge of import requirements in the buyer's country.

Rules for Sea and Inland Waterway Transport Only

FAS — Free Alongside Ship (named port of shipment): Risk passes when goods are placed alongside the vessel. For non-containerised (bulk or break-bulk) cargo only.

FOB — Free on Board (named port of shipment): Risk passes when goods are loaded on board the vessel. For non-containerised cargo and full container loads (FCL). Not recommended for LCL or air freight.

CFR — Cost and Freight (named port of destination): Seller pays freight to destination port; risk passes at loading port. For non-containerised cargo. Not recommended for containerised freight.

CIF — Cost, Insurance and Freight (named port of destination): As CFR, but seller also arranges insurance to destination port. For non-containerised cargo. Not recommended for containerised freight.

For the complete Incoterms 2020 guidance, including detailed rules and commentary, the official publication is available from the International Chamber of Commerce at iccwbo.org.

Epilogue: Never Stop Learning

This book began with a mantra, and it ends with the same one:

"You don't know what you don't know."

In the years since I first articulated that principle — in courtrooms, in negotiations, in conversations with traders who had just learned an expensive lesson — I have never found a more concise description of the central challenge of international trade.

The world changes. Tariff rates change. Trade agreements come and go. Markets open and close. Banking systems evolve. Technology disrupts supply chains and creates new ones. The cargo lawyer of the 1990s had never heard of blockchain. The exporter of 2015 had not anticipated the pandemic-driven disruption to global shipping in 2020 and 2021. The trader planning a market entry today faces a geopolitical landscape — sanctions, technology controls, reshoring trends, and shifting trade alliances — that would have been unrecognisable a decade ago.

What does not change is the need to know what you do not know — and to have the discipline and the intellectual honesty to keep asking that question, even after you are experienced.

The entrepreneur who builds a successful export business does not do so by mastering every detail of every market they operate in. They do it by building a team of people who collectively know more than any individual can, by maintaining relationships with specialists who can be called upon when the unexpected arises, and by cultivating the judgment to recognise the difference between a manageable risk and one that is genuinely beyond their capacity.

And they do it by keeping going. International trade is not for the faint-hearted, but it is enormously rewarding for those who persist. The relationships built across cultures and continents are among the most enduring in business. The satisfaction of shipping a cargo successfully, receiving payment promptly, and building a commercial presence in a market that a few years earlier seemed impossibly remote is real, and significant, and available to any trader who prepares carefully, acts prudently, and learns from every experience.

Be bold. Be rigorous. Be humble.

And never stop learning.

John Gates
Brisbane, Queensland, Australia

Acknowledgments

This book has been shaped by many people over many years.

To the team at SGS, where I spent time working with the world's largest inspection and testing company and learned first-hand how goods travel and why they sometimes don't arrive as intended: thank you for a practical education that no textbook could replicate.

To Professor Robert Grime and Professor John Wilson, two of my great instructors at the Institute of Maritime Law at the University of Southampton, whose books remain classics of international trade and shipping law: your influence is present throughout this work.

To the many clients, colleagues, and counterparts I encountered in practice and in business, both those whose deals went well and those who came to me after they had not: every one of those interactions contributed something to this book.

To the team at the International Trade Centre for making their model contracts freely available to small and medium enterprises who need them most.

To Steve Dickinson and the team at the China Law Blog for the clarity and precision of their writing on Chinese commercial law.

And to the many traders — the entrepreneurs who backed themselves, had a go, and kept going — who are the reason this book exists: may you always know a little more than you thought you did

About the Author

John Gates is an International Trade and Transport Lawyer, writer, and former Naval Officer based in Brisbane, Queensland. He has practised law in the fields of international trade, cargo claims, admiralty, and transport law, many years in general commercial law, and has spent time working with one of the world's largest inspection and testing organisations. He publishes under his own imprint, John Gates Books, as part of the International Trade and Transport Law Library series.

His legal textbook, Bills of Lading in Shipping Law: An Australian Perspective (Book Two in this series), provides detailed legal analysis of bills of lading and related matters under Australian law, including the Carriage of Goods by Sea Act 1991 (Cth) and the Hague-Visby Rules.

The next book will address the complex subject of Marine Insurance and there will be further works in the series.

He is also developing a fiction series for fun, enjoyment and curiosity, as well as enjoying his passion and obsession with the wonderful game of Rugby, and can be contacted at mediagate.jg@gmail.com

Made in the USA
Monee, IL
11 November 2026

161ec315-c65e-4c93-9cb7-d29a42787587R01

STEVE SIMON

THE **REPUBLICANS**

CHARTA

Design
Gabriele Nason
with Daniela Meda

Editorial Coordination
Filomena Moscatelli

Editing
Charles Gute

Copywriting and Press Office
Silvia Palombi Arte&Mostre, Milano

Web Design and Online Promotion
Barbara Bonacina

Cover
Red Hot—August 30, 2004, 23:21:06

ISBN 88-8158-561-8

Edizioni Charta
via della Moscova, 27
20121 Milano
Tel. +39-026598098/026598200
Fax +39-026598577
e-mail: edcharta@tin.it
www.chartaartbooks.it

Printed in Italy

To see more work by Steve Simon, go to
www.stevesimonphoto.com

An archive of articles and essays by
Mark Engler is available online at
www.DemocracyUprising.com

Having a book published is a rare and collaborative effort. For their constructive criticism and friendship I would like to thank Bree Seeley, Michael Regnier, Marc Rochette, Lesley Sparks, Lorraine Monk, Jill Delaney, JoAnne Stober, Ethan Eisenberg, Jason Eskenazi, Andrew Stawicki and PhotoSensitive, Katja Heinemann, Rita Leistner, John Trotter, Andy Levin, Margaret Williamson, Peter Bregg, Yuri Dojc, Chris Schwarz, Ben Rondel, Bob Todrick, Larry Wong, Greg Southam, Shaughn Butts, Andre Chitayat, Andrew Tolson, Bill White, Frank O'Connor and Doug Wicken.

Mark Engler, for his insightful observations on the convention and my work.

For their guidance, inspiration and support: Moises Saman, David Friend, Kathy Ryan, Elisabeth Biondi, Stacey Clarkson, Teri Boyd, Laurel Fischtein, Goldie Konopny, Sharon Fischtein, Martha Hanna, Pierre Dessureault, Jean-François Leroy, Delphine Lelu, Aaron Milrad, Saul Lederman, André Souroujon, Erin O'Connell, Elda Harrington, Paula Harrington, Beatriz Ventura, Graciela Smith, Guadalupe Molina, Alicia Méndez, Horacio Paone, Juan Travnik, Mary Virginia Swanson, MaryAnn Camilleri, Alison Nordstrom, Marilyn Simms, Amanda Gillespie, Jay DeFoore, Tina Schelhorn, and Barry Kirsh.

Giuseppe Liverani, Filomena Moscatelli, Daniela Meda and the staff at Charta in Milan—who believed in the work and made this book possible.

Of course, Frances Simon, Mac Simon, Teresa Simon, Dan Rennick, Joel Breslof, Judy and Larry Anderson, The Marcus Family, Phyllis Bailey, and Tanja Rohweder.
With love and gratitude.

Steve Simon, September 2005, New York City

Contents

INTRODUCTION: THE REPUBLICANS IN NEW YORK CITY

Mark Engler

When it came time for New Yorkers to vote, the decision was overwhelming. By a 3-to-1 margin they rejected the incumbent President of the United States, George W. Bush, and his vision for America. If the Republicans held their National Convention in New York in order to persuade the city's residents to join their cause, they had failed terribly.

Of course, the Republicans did not select the city because of a like-minded citizenry. They didn't want the actual New York, with all its diversity and creative energy. They came because of 9/11. They came to take the memory of the city's public grieving and to project it on screen as the backdrop for their political ambition.

Doing this was not altogether easy. It required them, first, to conceal some of their own feelings. Just months before the attacks that destroyed the World Trade Center, *The New York Times* reported, "Mr. Bush has been heard to say privately that he cannot stand New York." After 9/11, televangelist Jerry Falwell said, "I really believe that the pagans, and the abortionists, and the feminists, and the gays and the lesbians who are actively trying to make that an alternative lifestyle, the ACLU, People For the American Way, all of them who have tried to secularize America. I point the finger in their face and say, 'you helped this happen.'"

It's no secret where many such people live. In the view of the cultural right, New York City, a haven of liberalism and immigration, is a corrupted place.

The Republicans, then, had to keep out of the camera eye all those who weren't convinced of the sincerity of Falwell's later apology. When 5,000 delegates arrived in the city, they were greeted by more than 400,000 protesters, who marched as part of the largest demonstration in American history ever to confront a national political convention. The New York that presented itself—the two men who embraced near 34th Street, their lips pressed together; the woman at Ground Zero whose tank top expressed her views with characteristic directness: "Fuck Bush"—this city was not suitable. The Republicans would need to create their own New York.

* * *

Over 10,000 police officers were put in service for the convention, a large number of them charged with making Madison Square Garden a sealed fortress. Like photographer Steve Simon, I was among the journalists who passed from the protests into the rarefied space inside the arena. I showed my press badge, walked under the metal detector, and entered a different land. The Republicans I spoke with there were unfailingly polite and friendly, eager to talk with me even when I expressed disagreement with their militarism and their moralism. When prime-time speakers took the stage, I saw the delegates beam with enthusiasm and joy.

I see these delegates again in Steve Simon's images. Their faces are hopeful and often serene. They look into a future of common purpose and values. They are sympathetic: The three boys, dressed in their suits, standing with their prayerful mother. I could be the one in the middle, and that could be my younger brother on the right.

Yet you can also see something troubling in the photos. Something about the young people celebrating—maybe it is their haircuts, or their cuff links—makes the arena start to feel less welcoming. You look at them again and consider that these are the next generation of Republican leaders. You grow more aware that underneath the civility of the gathering, there is power.

Then you see: almost out of view, above the Presidential Seal, sits Bob Dole and, next to him, George H.W. Bush, the father. You glance to a different part of the arena and see another white-haired man in a suit. You realize it is Jerry Falwell himself, seated casually amidst an almost-empty row of chairs in Section 104.

* * *

One of Simon's photographs shows a procession of demonstrators carrying 1,000 flag-draped caskets through the streets of New York. On the sunny afternoon of that protest, I, too, was struck by the sight of those iconic coffins. The march moved slowly, and it stretched block after block. For over twenty minutes, I sat on the curb at 17th and Broadway and watched the pallbearers pace by.

The photo is a reminder, not only of the ultimate consequences of the convention's grandstanding, but also, in a time when media coverage of soldiers' coffins returning to U.S. military bases is banned, of the limits on what scenes are allowed to be a part of our political lives.

While some 15,000 journalists came to cover the Republicans, convention organizers took great pains to control "the message" these interpreters would take from the assembly. Operatives transcribed even the most ostensibly heartfelt sentiments onto jumbo teleprompters ("Almighty God… Together we laud and magnify your holy name…"). Most of the reporters, in turn, dutifully framed their dispatches around the key words posted on the walls of the auditorium ("A Safer World," "A Nation of Courage").

Steve Simon behaves differently. He shows us the staging off-camera and television personalities before they compose their august on-air expressions. He gives us the blur of the secret service removing an unwanted dissident from the arena; he shows the police scrutinizing the credentials of a father whose placard says something very different from the evening's preferred theme, "People of Compassion." It says, "Bush Lied. My Son Died."

Inside that arena, Simon is an unusual type of spy, one who records information others regard as irrelevant. He sneaks behind the broadcast booths, stepping over thick cables, and from the shadowy, quiet hollow he frames a shot of the wiring pinned to the news anchors' backs. Instead of jostling with other photographers for position on the convention floor, he includes the throng as his subject. In the stands, when everyone rises, eyes fixed on the stage, Steve Simon looks the other way, observing how deep rows of captivated faces fade into the dark recesses of the auditorium.

The photos that result do not recall the event as it was presented and understood. The medium allows a different story. Simon's art takes those instants of excitement and fear that marked the convention and holds them in place. Looking at his photos, I remember the intensity surrounding the jubilant Republicans, as well as the playfulness and despair that commingled in the demonstrations. I feel these things again. But now I have the opportunity to linger in these sensations without feeling self-conscious that I stay seated as the delegates jump up and pound their hands in applause, and without worrying about the police down the block who approach with plastic handcuffs. I realize how confined I felt during that week, which all the while we were told was a celebration of our freedoms.

The delegates now are elsewhere. The election is over. Yet we live still in an age when public debate is carefully choreographed, under a government that prizes control. In this setting, in these times, Simon's images remain renegade.

THE **REPUBLICANS**

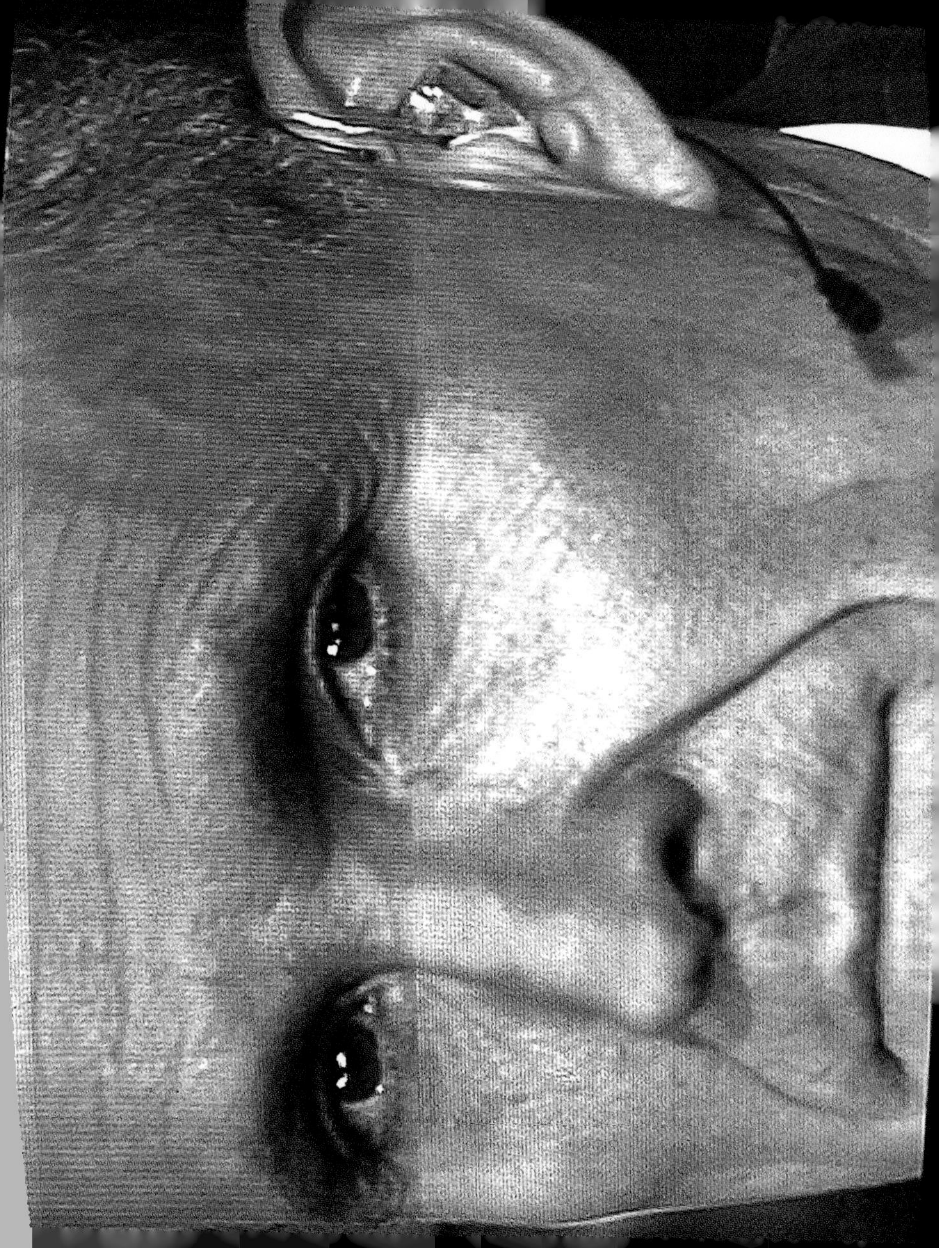

BOOTH 2

MADISON SQUARE G
REPUBLICAN NATIONAL CONVENTION
2004
NEW YORK

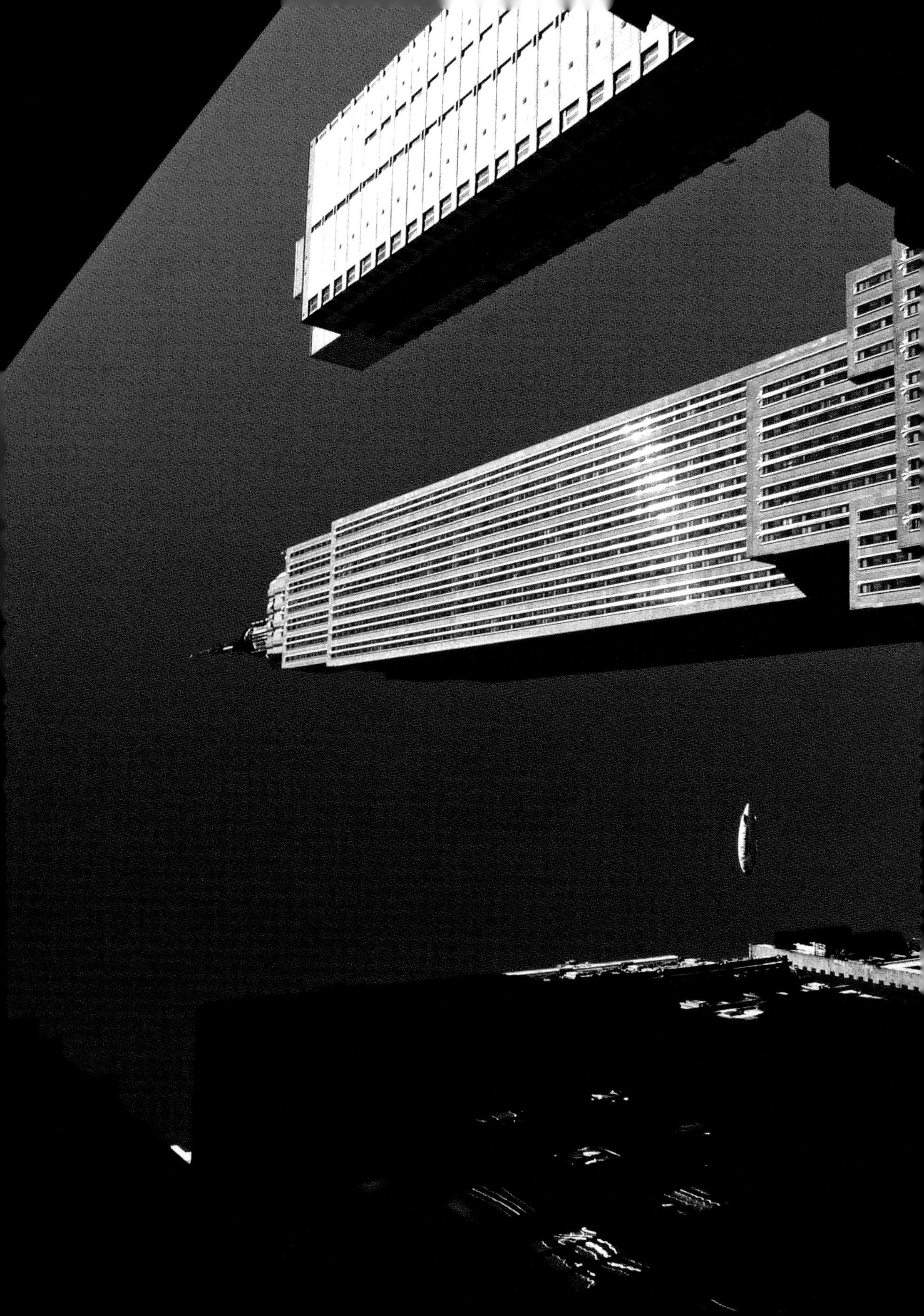

ice
WORKER
MARCH
BUSH
LIES
BOMBS AW
OUR CIT
SAY
TO TH
WA
ECON
NOYES

PORT 62
PORT 61
PORT 79
PORT 78
PORT 77
PORT 95
PORT 94
PORT 93

FLATRON
191 Benediction
TADA
Almighty God...
Together we laud
and magnify your
holy name...
LG

EFUL AMERICA
INTEGRITY
COURAGE
TRUST IN GOD
03

INTERNATIONAL
CNN
enEspañol
PBS
HOUR
PBS
NEWS
FOX

CNN
AMERICA VOTES
2004

Not one more day.
Not one more death.
Not one more deception.
END THE OCCUPATION OF IRAQ
united for peace & justice
END US SUPPORT FOR ISRAEL'S OCCUPATION
END THE OCCUPATION

NY
1

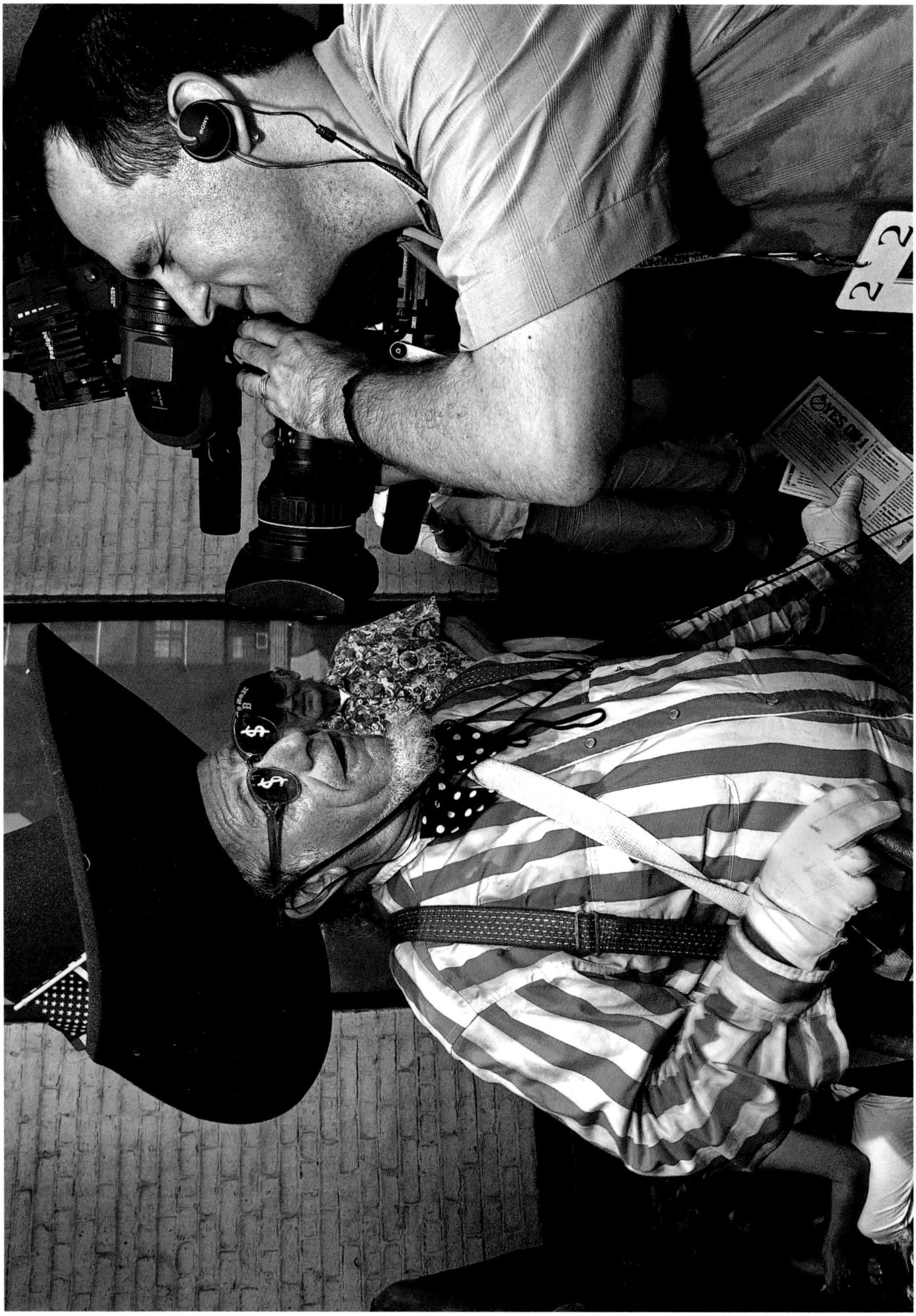

RONALD WILSON REAGAN
RONALD WILSON REAGAN
AN AMERICAN HERO
CNN
ScharffWeisberg
ScharffWeisberg

PEOPLE
COMPASS
COLORADO
WASHI
OK
OK
119
120
120

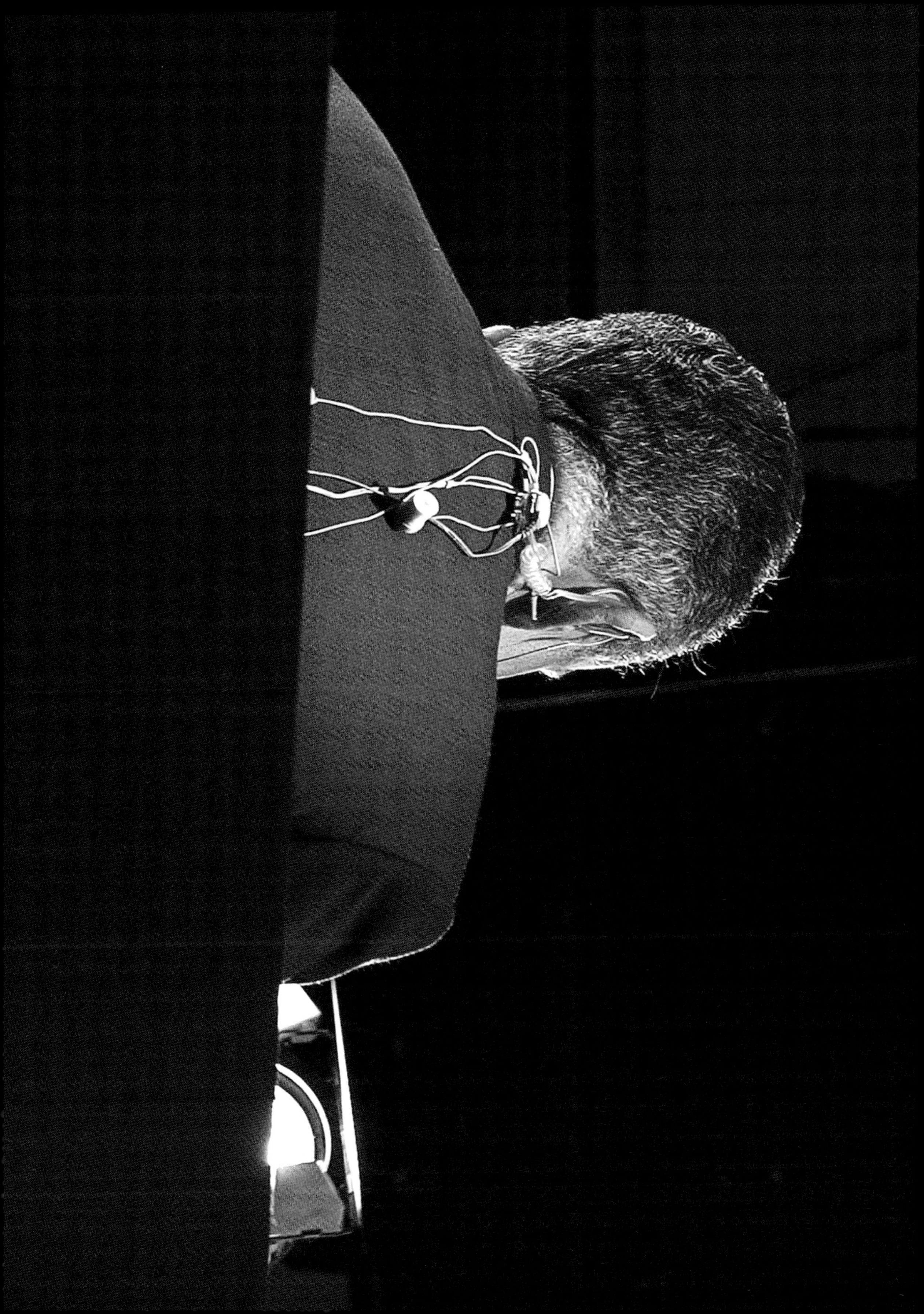

FLATRON
the OTHER party
says there ARE
TWO Americas.
believe THAT
LG

EXIT
105
49
106
50
Lori
Snuffer
West Virginia
4
MORE

SMASH THE
APARTHEID
WALL
Palestine Activist Forum of NY
TING BODIES
W
MADISON SQUARE GARDEN
FOX NEWS channel
AMERICA'S NEWSROOM
united for peace & justice

OUR TROO
A NATION OF
COURAGE
GO!
BUSH
A NATION OF
COURAGE
A NATION OF
COURAGE
I'M A
RED HOT
REPUBLICAN

$10

10

I ♥ PRO CHOICE NY
NARAL Pro-Choice New York
www.ProChoiceNY.org
PRO CHOICE NY
MAKE LOVE NOT LAW REVIEW

Every day 3.200 more
Americans are lost to
the terror of Abortion

REPUBLICAN
MASSACHUSETTS
WARNING – BUSH BITES BACK!
WASHINGTON
abcNEWS
Dubya
Lovya Dobya
Coors

FUCK BUSH

A SAFER WOR
A MORE HOPEF
AMERICA

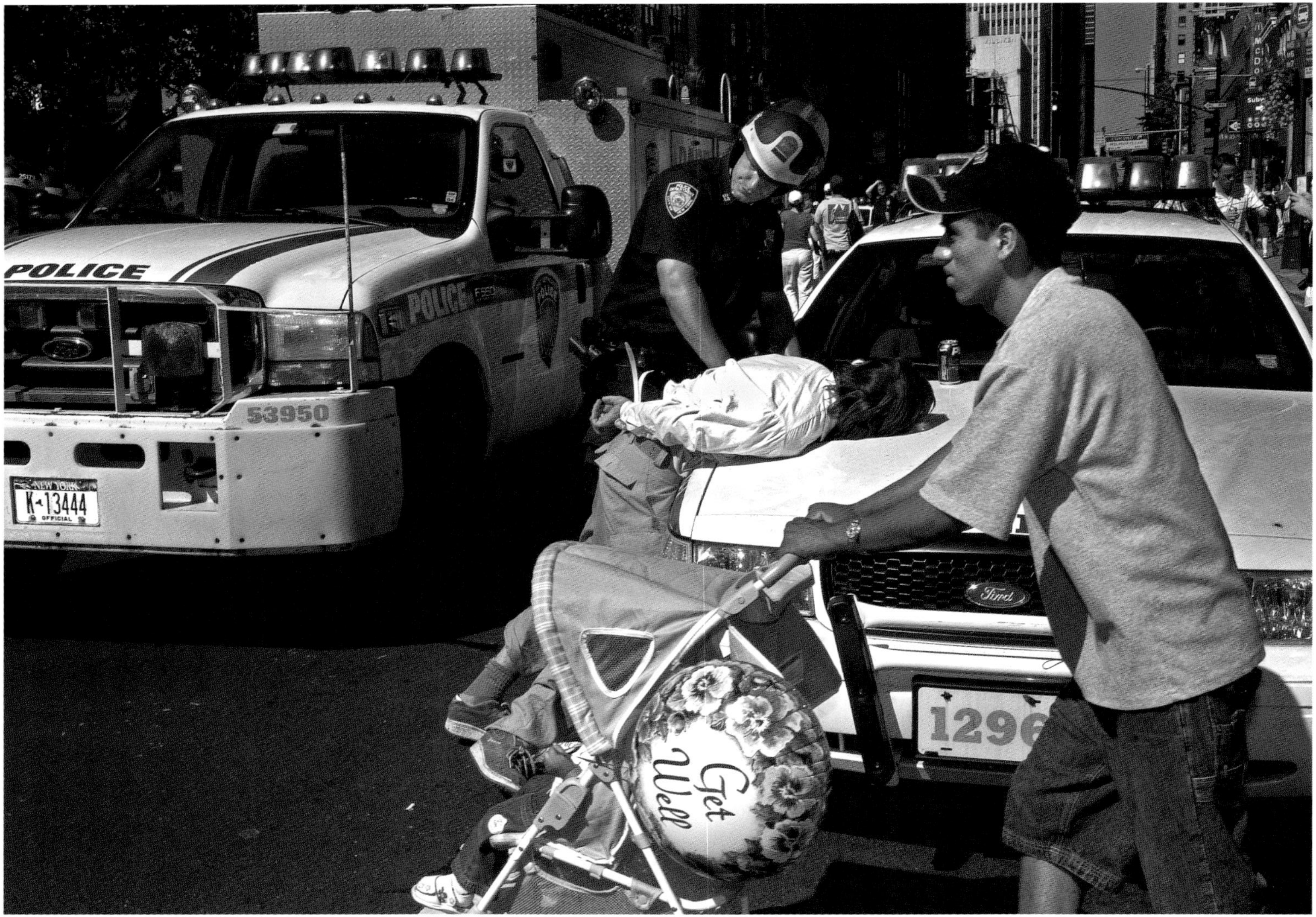
POLICE
POLICE
53950
NEW YORK
K-13444
OFFICIAL
Get Well

Republican National Convention 2004
NEXTEL
Republican National Convention 2004

4 More
Haitian Americans for Bush
KEEP BUSH ON TOP
My Heroes have always been Cowboys
VIVA BUSH
BUSH CHENEY
ONE MAN ONE WOMAN
verizon

الجزيرة
الجزيرة

RNC

SECTION 103
PEOPLE OF COMPASSION

WHO
BUSH
LIED
ABOUT
LIAR
Liberation
At Last!
Stop
NO
Coming
Fall 2004
WELCOME TO
NEW YORK
THAT SMELL
BUSH
Kodak
CAMERA

CHA

0:44:28
18min
48min
16BIT

e reade
PHARMACY WITHIN
SKIN CARE
BODY MASSAGE
THEATER
citibank

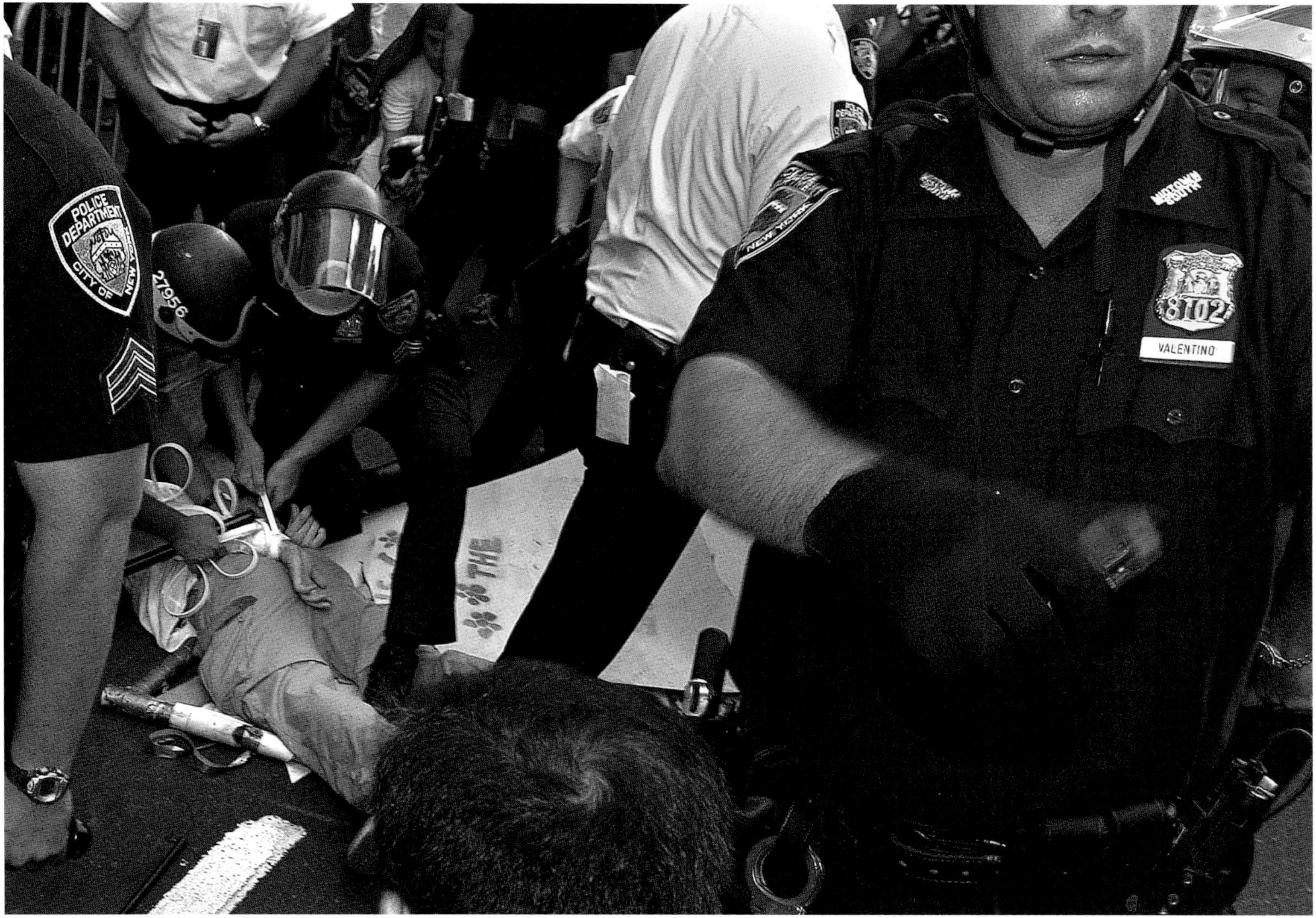
POLICE DEPARTMENT
CITY OF NEW YORK
27956
THE
8102
VALENTINO
MIDTOWN SOUTH

SEAL OF THE PRESIDENT OF THE UNITED STATES
E PLURIBUS UNUM
4
MORE
PEOPLE
OF

Thank you.
God Bless this
great country and
God Bless George
W. Bush.

4
MORE
NEW

The New York Times
The Republicans
THE CONVENTION IN NEW YORK
A Criminal Investigation
10
The Festivities Begin
16

List of Works

Make-up—August 30, 2004
13:53:41
p. 42

Protester Arrested—September 1, 2004
22:31:00
p. 43

Jesus/Twin Towers—August 27, 2004
18:08:35
pp. 44–45

Pro-Choice—August 28, 2004
14:01:00
p. 46

Anti-Abortion—August 28, 2004
13:45:16
p. 47

Posing—September 1, 2004
20:04:12
p. 48

Interviewed—August 28, 2004
18:57:51
p. 49

Safer World—September 2, 2004
19:30:29
p. 50

Fire—August 29, 2004
14:58:25
p. 51

Get Well—August 29, 2004
15:14:14
p. 52

Phone Calls—September 2, 2004
23:49:14
p. 53

4 More—August 31, 2004
21:23:15
p. 54

Al-Jazeera—August 29, 2004
12:39:18
p. 55

Edward Koch—August 30, 2004
18:21:26
pp. 56–57

Compassion—August 31, 2004
20:07:22
p. 58

Reflection—August 30, 2004
22:15:15
p. 59

Bush—August 31, 2004
21:25:14
p. 60

Lincoln—August 30, 2004
22:47:07
p. 61

Picture Taken—August 29, 2004
12:31:56
p. 62

Bush Mask—August 29, 2004
13:47:15
p. 63

Mother—August 30, 2004
23:07:06
p. 64

Father—August 31, 2004
23:23:15
p. 65

Flag Viewfinder—August31, 2004
20:21:00
p. 66

Mock Funeral—August 29, 2004
16:30:59
p. 67

Cheney Departs—August 30, 2004
20:35:52
p. 68

Arrest—August 29, 2004
15:07:45
p. 69

Bush Purse—September 2, 2004
20:41:11
p. 70

Presidential Seal—August 31, 2004
20:26:49
p. 71

God Bless Bush—September 1, 2004
22:18:18
p. 72

George W. Bush—September 2, 2004
23:17:24
p. 73

Boots—August 30, 2004
12:41:12
p. 75

All works are 17x22 inches, printed
digitally on archival fine art paper.

Appendix

Steve Simon was born in Montreal in 1960.

He is based in New York City.

Selected Solo Exhibitions

2005
The Republicans, Gallery One, Toronto
America At The Edge, Museo Fine Arts - Rafaela, Santa Fé

2004
America At The Edge, Escuela Argentina De Fotografia, Buenos-Aires
Empty Sky—The Pilgrimage To Ground Zero, RealTime Gallery, Toronto

2003
America At The Edge, BloWup Photogalerie, Montreal
Happy Birthday: Canada Days, Contact Photo Festival, Gallery One, Toronto

2002
Allegiance, The Half King, New York

1996
Healing Waters—The Pilgrimage To Lac Ste. Anne, Edmonton Art Gallery, Edmonton, Canada

Selected Group Exhibitions

2005
Water, Allen Lambert Galleria-BCE Place, Toronto
Contemporary American Photography—International Fototage, Mannheim / Ludwigshafen, Germany
Focused, Photographic Center Northwest, Seattle, Washington
Montreal en Priere / Festival Montreal en Lumiere, Downtown Montreal Winter Festival, Montreal

2004
HIV-Positive Zambia, University of North Dakota, Grand Forks, North Dakota

2003
Documents and Dreams, B'fly Gallery, Vancouver
Montreal At A Glance, Dorval Airport, Montreal
Amnesty International Photo Show & Silent Auction, Pikto Gallery, Toronto
Destination Toronto, B'fly Gallery, Vancouver
America At The Edge, Visa Pour L'Image Projection, Perpignan, France
Je Suis Montreal, outdoor exhibition, Montreal